STOPPING THE CONTINENT GRAB
AND THE REDD-IFICATION OF AFRICA

STOPPING THE CONTINENT GRAB AND THE REDD-IFICATION OF AFRICA

No REDD in Africa Network

Published by the
No REDD in Africa Network
http://no-redd-africa.org

The NO REDD in Africa Network (NRAN) is a collective of African civil society and community-based organizations and individuals opposed to all forms of REDD and REDD-type projects. NRAN sees REDD as a false climate solution that merely permits polluters to pollute and further harm the climate. We work to defend forest-dependent communities while promoting community-based forest protection. NRAN works with similar networks and groups in other regions of the world.

Contacts:

Justica Ambiental (JA!)
Maputo, Mozambique
E-Mail: anabela.ja.mz@gmail.com

Health of Mother Earth Foundation (HOMEF)
Benin City, Nigeria
E-mail: home@homef.org

ISBN-13: 978-1519104472
ISBN-10: 1519104472

Cover design: Cassandra Productions
http://www.cassandraproductions.net/
Design and layout: Tidiane Oumar BA - SOGO BA
http://www.sogoba.net/

CONTENTS

APPENDICES

1. Introduction: A call to decolonize Africa

The worst form of slavery is to willingly offer yourself on the auction block, get bought and pretend you are free. This is what participation in the mechanism called Reducing Emissions from Deforestation and Forest Degradation (REDD) is. Coming at a time when climate action has shifted away from legally binding requirements to voluntary, "intended nationally determined contributions", REDD provides a perfect space for polluters to keep polluting while claiming they are champions of climate action.

The REDD mechanism is already resulting in the violation of individual rights, as well as collective rights of communities and indigenous peoples. REDD offers polluting industries, carbon speculators, and governments that serve them the freedom to continue officially endorsed misbehavior.

This publication by the *No REDD in Africa Network* aims to demystify REDD and REDD-type projects, and all their variants, and show them for what they are: unjust mechanisms designed to usher in a new phase of colonization of the African continent. From examples presented, it is clear that the REDD mechanism is a scam and the polluters know that they are buying the "right" to pollute.

This briefing highlights the seriousness of the threat of the carbon trading Pandora's box being opened by REDD and REDD-type projects and shows clearly that what is in the offing is not just land or water grabs but a continental grab. REDD is not just another scramble for Africa, but a vicious grabbing of the entire continent, with those selling out demanding to be applauded for doing so in the name of "sustainable development". REDD is on course to result in grossly oppressive and exploitative systemic and structural changes which include a historic takeover of land tenure and water tenure, carbon colonialism, carbon slavery and exacerbated forms of violence against women.

REDD constitutes a new offensive against the peoples of Africa, especially farmers, pastoralists, hunter-gatherers and indigenous peoples.

REDD is a devious mechanism whose name sells what it cannot deliver. Everyone desires an end to deforestation and no one approves of forest degradation. REDD takes advantage of the critical role forests and all other ecosystems play in the ecological balance of Earth to sell the concept, while at the same time giving climate criminals the opening to enclose the commons, abridge community rights and gamble away our future through African carbon stock markets such as the African Carbon Exchange (ACX) in Kenya and the African Carbon Credit Exchange (ACCE) in Zambia.

The *No REDD in Africa Network* warns that REDD may be the ultimate wedge to crack open the door for the invasion of the African continent with genetically modified crops and trees. It could also promote the false notion that genetically modified crops are "climate smart" agriculture. It threatens to take over soils, water (blue carbon) and entire eco-systems. It may also rekindle the culture of colonial plantation agriculture also infamously called 'cash cropping'. In Africa, REDD is emerging as a new form of colonialism, economic subjugation, and impoverishment.

Outraged by the rampant land grabs and neocolonialism of REDD, Africans at the World Social Forum in Tunisia in 2013 took the historic decision to launch the *No REDD in Africa Network* to defend the continent from the REDD onslaught.[1] Through this publication the *No REDD in Africa Network* is calling for a decolonization of Africa and the building of hope for present and future generations. This is a timely call we must all heed. We cannot stay silent while a whole generation of landless Africans is being created on the platform of a climate scam.

2. What is REDD?

In this book we refer to a range of mechanisms – as REDD (including REDD+ and REDD-type projects) that have been developed within and outside the United Nations system ostensibly to deal with deforestation and climate change. REDD has been under negotiation within the United Nations Framework Convention on Climate Change (UNFCCC) since 2005. The stated objective of the negotiations is to reduce net global emissions of greenhouse gases by controlling forest management in developing countries.

The box below from GRAIN summarizes how the mechanism is meant to work:

What is REDD+?[2]

REDD stands for **R**educing **E**missions from **D**eforestation and Forest **D**egradation in developing countries. It is the term under which forest loss is discussed at United Nations (UN) climate meetings. Since 2005, the issue of forest loss has distracted governments at these UN meetings from addressing the real cause of climate change – turning ancient underground deposits of oil, coal and gas into fossil fuels and burning them. Instead of coming up with a plan on how to end the release of greenhouse gas emissions that is the consequence of burning these fossil fuels, the UN climate talks have spent much time debating deforestation of tropical forests. Of course it is important to halt forest loss, also because of the CO_2 emissions that are released when forests are destroyed. But reducing deforestation is no substitute for coming up with a plan on how to stop burning fossil fuel! The trouble with REDD is that that is exactly its consequence: enabling industrialised countries to burn fossil fuels a little longer.

REDD+ is another word the UN uses to discuss forests, and the plus stands for "enhancing carbon stocks, sustainable forest management

---

and forest conservation" – or, as one commentator stated, "at some stage someone thought it fitting to tag on the "+" which would come to represent all those other things that have come to the attention of the international development industry in recent years (like conservation, gender, indigenous people, livelihoods and so on)". REDD was originally designed for countries with high deforestation, Brazil and Indonesia in particular. This meant that funding would be available primarily for those countries with much potential to reduce their rate of deforestation. Only eight countries accounting for 70% of tropical forest loss would thus be involved. Countries with much forest but little deforestation – Guyana, DRC, Gabon, for example – therefore insisted that REDD be designed so they would also have access to REDD funding, for example through being paid to not increase projected future deforestation. The plus was thus also added so that countries with low levels of deforestation but a lot of forest could also have access to what was at the time expected to be large sums of money for REDD+ activities.[3]

How is REDD+ meant to work?

Forest-rich countries in the global South agree to reduce emissions from forest destruction as part of a UN climate agreement. To demonstrate exactly how many tonnes of carbon (dioxide) have been saved, the government produces a national REDD+ plan, which explains how much forest **would have been** destroyed over the next few decades. Then they describe how much forest they would be willing not to cut if someone paid them to keep the forest standing. They calculate how much it would cost not to destroy this forest and how much carbon will not be released into the atmosphere as a result of keeping the forest intact.

In return, industrialised countries (or companies or international NGOs) pay the tropical forest countries (or individual REDD+ projects) to prevent the forest destruction that is claimed to happen without REDD+ finance. The payment will only be made if the forest country shows that forest loss has actually been reduced **and** that the carbon that otherwise would have been released into the atmosphere continues to be stored in the forest. That is why people sometimes talk about "results-based" or "performance" payments for REDD+. The REDD+ project also needs to show that without the REDD+ money the forest would have been destroyed. This last point is important because many industrialised countries and corporations that fund REDD+ activities want to receive something in return for their financial support. This something is called a *carbon credit* (the name might change in the UN climate treaty that governments are expected to adopt in Paris in December 2015). The WRM publication, "10 things communities should know about REDD"[4], explains why the calculations that create carbon credits are not credible and why it is impossible to know whether forest was really only saved because of the REDD+ money.

What is this carbon credit good for?

A carbon credit is essentially a right to pollute. A polluting country or company that has made a commitment to reduce their greenhouse gas emissions does not reduce their emissions by as much as they said they would. Instead, they pay someone elsewhere to make the reduction for them. That way, the polluter can claim to have lived up to their commitment when in reality they continue burning more oil and coal and release more CO_2 into the atmosphere than they said they would. At the other end of the (REDD+) carbon credit deal, someone claims they were planning to destroy a forest but as a result of the payment, they decided to not destroy that forest. The carbon saved by protecting the forest that otherwise would have been cut is sold as a carbon credit to the polluter who keeps burning more fossil fuels than agreed. In other words, the owner of the carbon credit has the right to release one tonne of fossil carbon they had promised to avoid because someone else has saved a tonne of carbon in a forest that without the carbon payment would have been destroyed, releasing CO_2. On the voluntary carbon market, where corporations and individuals buy carbon credits to claim that (some of) their emissions have been offset, REDD+ credits are traded for between US$3 and US$10.

Why does trading carbon credits not reduce emissions?

There are many problems with this idea of (carbon) offsets. Among them that they do not reduce overall emissions – what is saved in one place allows extra emissions in another place. In the case of REDD+ offsets, another problem is the very important difference between the carbon stored in oil, coal and gas and the carbon stored in forests. The carbon stored in the trees is part of a natural cycle through which carbon is constantly released and absorbed by plants. The terrestrial carbon has been circulating between the atmosphere, the oceans and the forest for millions of years.

Deforestation over the centuries has meant that too much of the carbon naturally in circulation has ended up in the atmosphere and too little in forests. Today, industrial agriculture, logging, infrastructure and mining are the main drivers of deforestation. When industrialised countries started burning oil and coal, they further increased the amount of carbon that could accumulate in the atmosphere. The carbon in these "fossil fuels" had been stored underground for millions of years, without contact with the atmosphere. Its release greatly increases the amount of carbon dioxide in the atmosphere, which in turn causes the climate to change. Although plants can absorb part of this additional carbon released from ancient oil and coal deposits, they do so only temporarily. When the plant dies or a forest is destroyed or burns, the carbon is released and increases the concentration of CO_2 in the atmosphere (adding to the imbalance from forest destruction).

That is why REDD+ credits not only don't help reduce overall emissions, but also will lead to an increase of CO_2 concentrations in the atmosphere, because REDD+ is built on the false assumption that forest and fossil carbon are the same when from a climate perspective they are clearly not!

3. A few more definitions

Take a deep breath. Inhale. Exhale. How does it feel to know that the air we breathe is being privatized? The atmosphere is becoming the private property of industry and governments through something called "carbon trading."

Carbon trading creates units of pollution in the form of metric tons of carbon dioxide and five other greenhouse gases, and sells them on stock markets called **carbon markets.**

The trade of these permits to pollute, known as carbon credits allows polluting industries and countries to cheaply and easily get out of obligations to reduce pollution at source. Carbon trading lets polluters off the hook. Carbon trading is premised on the takeover, commodification, privatization and sale of nature by financial markets known as the "financialization of nature" that underpins what is being called the "Green Economy".

The **'Green Economy'** is the umbrella for all kinds of ways to sell nature including REDD+, the Clean Development Mechanism, carbon trading, PES (Payment for Environmental Services), the financialization of nature, the International Regime on Access to Genetic Resources, patents on life, TEEB (The Economics of Ecosystems and Biodiversity), natural capital, green bonds, species banking and state and business 'partnerships' with indigenous peoples. Under the Green Economy, even the rain, the beauty of a waterfall or a honey-bee's pollen may be reduced to a barcode price tag and sold to the highest bidder. At the same time, the Green Economy promotes and *greenwashes* environmentally and socially devastating extractive industries like logging, mining and oil drilling as 'sustainable development'. Nothing could be further from the truth.

Carbon trading was invented by Richard Sandor and others in the 1980s[5] and is conducted by stock markets as well as under the auspices of the United

Nations, its UN Framework Convention on Climate Change (UNFCCC) and Kyoto Protocol. Carbon trading under the UN is on the "mandatory market" because it is done to comply with legally binding commitments to reduce emissions, and, hence, mandatory.

But individuals, companies and states can also buy and sell carbon credits outside the UN on the "voluntary market." Polluters use the voluntary market to accumulate carbon credits in anticipation of future requirements to reduce emissions, to "greenwash" their image or because they think it reduces global warming. There are carbon markets in Europe, Africa and Brazil and there are also many cases of carbon speculation, carbon fraud and even carbon "criminals".[6]

Under the UN's Clean **Development Mechanism** (CDM), carbon credits can also be obtained from projects in the Global South which supposedly reduce, avoid or capture carbon dioxide (CO_2) in order to compensate for or offset pollution elsewhere. These emissions compensations are called carbon offsets. Carbon offsets are generated from projects such as hydroelectric dams or tree plantations. The CDM outsources the obligation to reduce emissions to the Global South and has been denounced as carbon colonialism.

Trees absorb carbon dioxide and release oxygen thanks to photosynthesis. Photosynthesis is the premise of carbon offsets with forests. Ostensibly REDD is a mechanism to deal with climate change and protect forests by providing incentives through carbon offsets. The basic idea behind REDD is simple: developing countries that are willing and able to reduce emissions from deforestation should be financially compensated for doing so.

REDD developed from a proposal in 2005 by a group of countries in the UN called the Coalition for Rainforest Nations. In June 2015, after ten years of negotiations, the UN finalized REDD.[7] It is expected that REDD will be included in the outcome document of the UN's World Climate Summit held in Paris in December 2015.[8]

According to REDD Monitor, "The devil, as always, is in the details. The first detail is that the payments are not for keeping forests, but for reducing emissions from deforestation and forest degradation. This might seem like splitting hairs, but it is important, because it opens up the possibility, for example, of logging an area of forest but compensating for the emissions by planting industrial tree plantations somewhere else."[9]

Some of the key technical problems with REDD *are leakage, additionality, permanence and measurement.* These terms basically refer to all the tricky ways that REDD does not work because deforestation can be displaced; there is no way of proving a forest was going to get logged unless you can foresee the future; trees do not store carbon dioxide forever; and because no one really knows how to measure tree carbon let alone fully understands and can track and quantify the atmosphere's carbon cycle.

Leakage refers to the fact that while deforestation might be avoided in one place, the forest destroyers might move to another area of forest or to a different country.

Additionality refers to the near-impossibility of predicting what might have happened in the absence of the REDD project.

Permanence refers to the fact that carbon stored in trees is only temporarily stored. All trees eventually die and release the carbon back to the atmosphere.

Measurement refers to the fact that accurately measuring the amount of carbon stored in forests and forest soils is extremely complex – and prone to large errors." [10]

4. The evolution of REDD, REDD+ etc.

REDD's scope has been expanded beyond forests and now includes all land and coastal ecosystems. This expanded scope is indicated by the two plus signs after the acronym: REDD++.

Here is a breakdown of REDD's evolution.

REDD (Reducing Emissions from Deforestation and Forest Degradation)
Includes plantations
According to the United Nations, a 'forest' is any area bigger than 500 square meters with crown cover of 10 per cent and trees capable of growing two meters high. This means that not only the biodiverse forests like the Amazon and the Congo Basin are considered forests for REDD, but also millions of hectares of **monoculture tree** plantations are considered forests, too. REDD also includes what the UN calls "perverse incentives" to **cut down real forests** and replace them with plantations of invasive species like pine, eucalyptus, spruce or acacia.[11] The UN also allows for the use of genetically modified trees for REDD.[12]

REDD+
Includes more plantations and logging
REDD+ is REDD plus *conservation, sustainable management of forests and enhancing of carbon stocks.*

Here is an explanation of these concepts:

Conservation
Although forest conservation sounds good, the history of the establishment of national parks and protected areas includes massive evictions of indigenous peoples and local communities.[13] As a recent study shows, these parks and protected areas performed worse than community-managed forests in controlling deforestation.[14]

Sustainable forest management (SFM)

In the climate negotiations "sustainable forest management" is code for **logging**. It is worth noting that "temporally unstocked carbon" is code for **clear-cuts** and is also allowed under REDD.[15]

Enhancement of carbon stocks

Enhancing carbon stocks may be implemented through large-scale monoculture plantations with adverse impacts on biodiversity, forests and local communities.

Landscape REDD[16], as its names suggests, is REDD with the addition of entire landscapes and could include Climate Smart Agriculture, also a form of REDD with soils and agriculture, and even organic farming and agroecology.

For the purposes of this briefing, we will refer to all the variants of REDD as simply REDD. We will also use the term "REDD-type projects." REDD-type projects are not officially REDD projects but they use forest carbon to generate carbon credits and are indicative of what the impacts of REDD implementation may be. It is also worth noting that currently REDD is in what is called the "REDD readiness" phase but with the signing of the Paris Accord in December 2015, REDD may begin to enter into its implementation phase.

5. What does REDD mean in reality?

REDD, like carbon trading, is a false solution to climate change that is promoted by the United Nations, the World Bank and climate criminal corporations such as Shell[17], Chevron and Rio Tinto[18]. It allows polluters to continue to burn fossil fuels without any obligation to reduce their emissions at source. While REDD may be claimed to stand for 'Reducing Emissions from Deforestation and Forest Degradation', in practice REDD really means *Reaping profits from Evictions, land grabs, Deforestation and Destruction of biodiversity.*[19] REDD constitutes a worldwide land grab and gigantic carbon offset scam. Even the United Nations admits that REDD could result in the "lock-up of forests," "loss of land" and "new risks for the poor of the world."[20]

And when might the floodgates of this onslaught be open?

The year 2015 is when the legally binding Paris Accord will be signed at the United Nations World Climate Summit. The post-2015 development agenda has already been endorsed by member states in September during the United Nations General Assembly. These two major international frameworks advance the controversial Green Economy agenda which has been rejected by many civil society groups because it promotes the financialisation of nature through the use of REDD and other market-based schemes.

Implementation of the Paris Accord will most likely begin in 2020. However, the New York Declaration on Forests adopted at the UN in 2014 calls for REDD before and after 2020. "Bankability" of carbon credits may allow for REDD credits to be accumulated in the coming years while they are relatively cheap, stockpiled or "banked" and then used when implementation is in full swing.

The principal REDD promoters include industrialized countries like Norway, the European Union, the United States, Australia, Japan, China and Brazil as well the State of California. Alongside national governments, multinational and trans-national corporations from the extractive, logging, agro-chemical, and pulp and paper industries are leading the charge.

The graphic below "Who benefits from REDD? Players and Power" provides a snapshot of who is behind REDD and reveals that far from protecting forests, most REDD promoters are destroying forests and the environment.

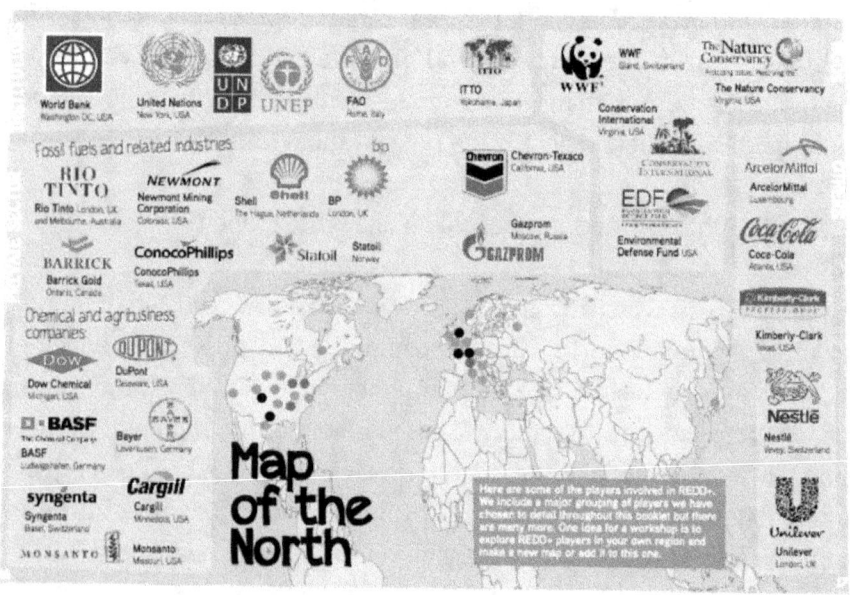

Source: Who benefits from REDD? Players and Power[21] Carbon Trade Watch and Indigenous Environmental Network

Frontlines of REDD in the World

It is helpful to begin to visualize REDD's expansion in terms of geography. Since REDD initially focused on grabbing control of the world's forests, it is useful to look at where the principal forest ecosystems are found. It would be important to do a similar mapping exercise with the world's fertile land,

Landscape REDD and Climate Smart Agriculture to calculate the total amount of land that may be grabbed through these mechanisms.

The following map shows where the world's most important remaining forests are found. All three of these forest systems are priorities for the Green Economy, not just in terms of securing the land for REDD credits.

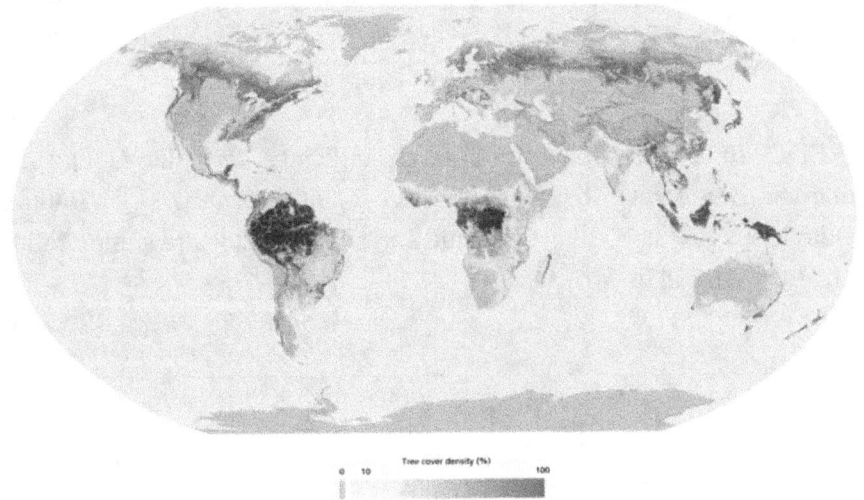

World Forest 2010 Map[22]

Impacts of REDD

The impacts of REDD in Africa include massive land grabs, carbon colonialism, servitude and carbon slavery, threats to cultural survival, violent evictions, at least one killing, huge plantations, persecution and criminalization of activists, corruption, carbon scams and crooks, and corporate greenwash.

These impacts have been documented by the *No REDD in Africa Network* in *The Worst REDD-type Projects in Africa* as well as by groundbreaking reports such as the exposé on the N'hambita Project by La Via Campesina, and Timberwatch's case study of CDM Carbon Sink Plantations in Tanzania.[23]

It is also worthwhile to review the Friends of the Earth-France's report on Air France and REDD+ in Madagascar[24] since airline REDD offsets are a growing trend and much of the supposed offsetting may be done in Africa.

A study is needed on the comparative costs of establishing and maintaining tree plantations by region to verify if it is cheapest to do such offsets in Africa, and, if, therefore, there is more pressure to grab land for REDD and to "tree-ify" Africa than other regions. In this regard, the GPL REDD Report anticipates that a large part of REDD is expected to happen in Africa.[25]

No REDD In Africa Network research indicates that the Congo Basin (Cameroon, Democratic Republic of Congo, Congo, Central Africa Republic), Uganda, Madagascar, Kenya, Tanzania and Mozambique are some of the key frontlines of REDD in Africa.

6. Characteristics of REDD-type projects in Africa

In 2013, the *No REDD in Africa Network* began building a database on REDD-type projects in Africa to start to compile a panoramic view of what was happening with REDD in the continent.

The initial findings of the database research served to inform the Network's first workshop held in Maputo in August of 2013 and to prepare the *No REDD in Africa Network's* summary of *The Worst REDD-type Projects in Africa.* [26] (An excerpt follows. All the pertinent references can be accessed at http://no-redd-africa.org/index.php/16-redd-players/84-the-worst-redd-type-projects-in-africa-continent-grab-for-carbon-colonialism).

This summary has proven to be important for illustrating the nature and gravity of the human rights abuses and the scale of the repression resulting from REDD-type projects. It was also helpful for beginning to sketch the scale of the land grab and coining of the term "Continent Grab" to describe the amount of African land at risk of REDD+-ification.

| UGANDA: Massive repression: 22,000 evicted |

Over 22,000 peasants, some with land titles were violently evicted from the Mubende and Kiboga districts in Uganda to make way for the UK-based New Forests Company to plant trees, to earn carbon credits and, ultimately, to sell the timber. According to *The New York Times*, "New Forests Company (NFC), grows forests in African countries with the purpose of selling credits from the carbon dioxide its trees soak up to polluters abroad." *The New York Times* also reports that "…[V]illagers described gun-toting soldiers and an 8-year-old child, [Friday Mukamperezida], burning to death when his home was set ablaze by security officers. New Forests Company is 20% owned by the HSBC bank, and investors in the project include the World Bank. Evicted successful farmers are reduced to becoming poorly paid plantation peons on the land they were evicted from. "Homeless and hopeless, Mr. Tushabe said he took a job with the company that pushed him out. He was promised more than $100 each month, he said, but received only about $30."NFC has been certified under the Forest Stewardship Council since 2009.

KENYA: Threats to cultural survival

Despite Amnesty International's recommendation to "stop immediately the practice of forced evictions," as Kenya's Mau Forest was made "ready" for a UNEP-funded REDD+ project, members of the Ogiek People suffered violent evictions, and Ogiek activists were attacked for protesting land grabs. Minority Rights Group International includes the Ogiek People in their list of "Peoples Under Threat" from genocide, mass killings or violent repression and this latest wave of evictions threatened the cultural survival of the Ogiek People. In March 2013, the African Court on Human and Peoples' Rights issued provisional measures to ensure that the Ogiek cannot be evicted while the case is before the court.

MOZAMBIQUE: Carbon Slavery

Envirotrade's N'hambita Community Carbon Project, a REDD project in Mozambique, constitutes multi-generational carbon slavery. For seven years, farmers receive an annual payment for as little as $63 per family to plant and tend trees to offset pollution in Europe and the US, but the contract stipulates that they must continue to do so for 99 years. In the event that the farmers die, their children and their children's children have to continue to take care of the trees for free. *The Africa Report* calls the N'hambita project "a clear case of carbon slavery." Furthermore, farmers are "growing" carbon instead of growing food. According to Via Campesina, this can undermine food security in the area, as farmers will dedicate time, labor and land to trees instead of sustenance. According to REDD Monitor, one of the two founders of Envirotrade, Robin Birley, was denounced by the South African Truth and Conciliation Commission "for arming and training a paramilitary group that was involved in destabilizing South Africa's first democratic election." A warrant for his arrest was issued in relation to a stockpile of weapons obtained from Eugene de Kock, a colonel in the apartheid-era South African police. Birley was also "president of the Mozambique Institute in the early 1990s, which supported RENAMO, the South African-backed force that systematically committed war crimes and crimes against humanity during the civil war in Mozambique." The other founder of Envirotrade, Phillip Powell bankrolled the Chilean dictator Augusto Pinochet's luxurious bail residence while his extradition from the United Kingdom was pending for charges of crimes against humanity. Nonetheless, the N'hambita Project has not been sanctioned but hailed as an inspiring model on the United Nations Rio+20 website and certified under the Climate, Community and Biodiversity Alliance Standard's Gold Level standard.

DEMOCRATIC REPUBLIC OF CONGO: Servitude

According to "The DRC Case Study: The impacts of carbon sinks of Ibi-Batéké Project on the Indigenous Pygmies of the Democratic Republic of Congo" published by the International Alliance of Indigenous and Tribal Peoples of the Tropical Forests, Batwa Pygmies suffer "servitude" on the World Bank Ibi-Batéké Carbon Sink Plantation. An employee of the project says "this must not be understood…as if it were slavery." This REDD-type forest carbon plantation for fuel wood and charcoal is the DRC's first Clean Development Project and claims to contribute to sustainable development and climate change mitigation. The World Bank hails it as a model for all of Africa. However, Pygmy leaders have repeatedly denounced the World Bank for funding deforestation of their ancestral forests, which not only releases emissions but also violates their rights, leads to the destruction of their livelihood and causes social conflict. Furthermore, according to "Advance Guard" published by the United Nations University, "Indigenous Peoples' rights, experiences, and cultural and spiritual traditions are being ignored. Nothing to ensure the Pygmy's preliminary consent, which was mandated within the framework of the project, has been done since consultation began."

DEMOCRATIC REPUBLIC OF CONGO: Losing rights to forests

Even Mickey Mouse is getting in on REDD. According to the World Rainforest Movement, the Walt Disney Company, Conservation International and Diane Fossey Gorilla Fund International are promoting a REDD pilot project on the Tayna Gorilla Reserve (RGT) and the Kisimba-Ikobo Primate Reserve (RPKI) in the Democratic Republic of Congo. In Kisimba and Ikobo, the REDD project is being developed against a backdrop of social conflicts sparked by opposition to the creation of the Kisimba-Ikobo Primate Reserve itself. The establishment of the reserve stripped local communities of their customary rights over the land and forests within its borders. Local communities such as the Bamate, Batangi and Bakumbule communities are losing their rights and control over their ancestral forests. Decisions related to the project are being made almost entirely without the knowledge of the local communities, who are supposedly meant to be the primary beneficiaries. Despite their right to free, prior and informed consent, communities may play only a marginal role in the decision-making process of the REDD project. The situation of women is even more troubling, because they are even less informed than the men and therefore cannot express any opinions or demands.

LIBERIA: Billion Dollar Carbon Scam

Liberian President Ellen Johnson Sirleaf established a commission to investigate a proposed forest carbon credit deal between the West African nation's Forest Development Authority (FDA) and UK-based Carbon Harvesting Corporation, which aimed to secure around a fifth of Liberia's total forest area — 400,000 hectares — in a forest carbon concession. Police in London arrested Mike Foster, CEO of Carbon Harvesting Corporation. Global Witness said the project potentially exposed the Liberian government to more than $2 billion in liabilities.

CHEVRON was sued for murder of Nigerians and does REDD with ARMED GUARDS in Brazil

Chevron was sued for participating in the murder, shooting and subsequent torture of Nigerian villagers engaging in environmental protest against the oil giant. For its destruction of the Amazon, Chevron was recently ordered by an Ecuadorian court to pay $19 billion in damages. Now, Chevron uses armed guards for a REDD-type project in Brazil. Chevron, The Nature Conservancy, General Motors, American Electric Power and the Society for Wildlife Research and Environmental Education have implemented the Guaraqueçaba Climate Action Project in the ancestral territory of Guarani People with uniformed armed guards called "Força Verde" or "Green Force" who intimidate and persecute local communities; jailing and shooting at people who go into the forest as well as forcibly entering and searching private homes without due authorization "…[T]he project has caused devastating impacts on the local communities…" and raises the specter of REDD militarization.

GREENWASHING SHELL'S ATROCITIES

Two of the biggest greenhouse polluters on the planet oil giants, Gazprom and Shell, infamous for the genocide of the Ogoni People and environmental destruction in Nigeria's Niger Delta, bankroll the Rimba Raya REDD project in Central Kalimantan, Indonesia. The project is also supported by the Clinton Foundation and approved by the Voluntary Carbon Standard (VSC) and Climate, Community and Biodiversity Alliance (CCBA). Nnimmo Bassey, the former Director of Environmental Rights Action (FoE-Nigeria) and Winner of the Alternative Nobel Prize, says, "We have suffered Shell's destruction of communities and biodiversity as well as oil spills and gas flaring for decades. Now we can add financing REDD for greenwash and profits to the long list of Shell's atrocities." Oilwatch recently denounced that Shell is trying to use REDD to "roast the planet." The Rimba Raya REDD project is more controversial than ever - even REDD promoters are fighting among themselves. Meanwhile, Shell is buying up and renaming forests in Canada as "Shell Forests" and pretending to offset its pollution for its refinery in Martinez, California with forests in the state of Michigan.

NIGERIA: Persecution and criminalization of activists

REDD is already contributing to the persecution and criminalization of activists, including in Cross River State, Nigeria where the World Bank, UN-REDD and the State of California intend to do REDD projects. Odey Oyama, Executive Director of the Rainforest Resource and Development Centre (RRDC) in Cross River State, Nigeria suffered harassment and intimidation from state security agents and had to flee his home for several weeks in the months of January and February 2013 for opposing REDD activities (aimed at extracting more forest estates from indigenous communities) and other similar land grab operations (e.g. for large scale plantation farming). "One of the activities placing me in confrontation with the Cross River State Government of Nigeria is my stand against the REDD programme. My reason for rejecting the REDD programme is because it is geared towards taking over the last vestiges of community forest that exist in Cross River State of Nigeria," denounced Mr. Oyama.

UGANDA: Carbon colonialism

In Uganda, a carbon credit tree plantation project in the Mount Elgon National Park to absorb European pollution may have violently evicted as many as six thousand people, including the Indigenous Benet People, and destroyed crops and homes. The project entailed the Dutch FACE Foundation and the Uganda Wildlife Authority (UWA) proposing to plant 25,000 hectares of trees to supposedly offset emissions from air travel and a 600 MW coal-fired power station in the Netherlands. By 2006, only 8,500 hectares had been planted. Despite promises of employment, only a few seasonal jobs were created. Evictions occurred both for the national park and for the carbon offset project. After one of the evictions, "the evicted people were forced to move to neighboring villages where they lived in caves and mosques." According to a report in a local newspaper, in 2004, "Park rangers killed more than 50 people." Local communities have suffered evictions, human rights violations, loss of land, food, (including the traditional fare malewa (bamboo shoots)), income and livelihood. In 2002, the contracted assessor of the carbon offset project, Société Générale de Surveillance Agrocontrol (SGS), stated that in order for the tree-planting project to continue, "more people will have to be evicted." They even recommended that "more speed may be required to ensure the evictions are carried out successfully." The evictions from the National Park continued while the project was certified by the Forest Stewardship Council. According to World Rainforest Movement, "Villagers... have been beaten and shot at, have been barred from their land and have seen their livestock confiscated by armed park rangers guarding the 'carbon trees' inside the National Park... The 'offset' project sold carbon credits to Greenseat, a Dutch company with clients including Amnesty International, the British Council and the Body Shop." "[C]ommunities deliberately destroyed the trees – for them a symbol of their exclusion from land that was once theirs" and planted corn to eat. In 2005, the Supreme Court ruled in favor of communities vindicating their rights to live on their land and continue to farm.

TANZANIA: Conflict and corruption

The Tanzanian government has been "called to resolve land quarrels between two villages of Muungano and Milola Magharibi in Lindi District after their residents threatened to fight each other over benefits from forests. Speaking to The Guardian in Lindi recently, the villagers said their land disputes erupted after the Tanzania Community Forest Conservation Network (TCFCN) introduced a project on forest conservation in the area. The misunderstanding came to the surface after the organizers of the project announced that the village that will conserve a large area of the forest will get more money for the Reduction of Emissions from Deforestation and forest Degradation (REDD)."

REDD AGRICULTURE: SOIL CARBON – Selling the Earth

REDD+ is not just done with forests and plantations, but with soils, fields and agriculture as well. Agricultural carbon offsets also called Climate Smart Agriculture could threaten communities, farms and food security, cause hunger and even make climate change worse. According to La Via Campesina, the world's largest peasant movement, "soil carbon markets could also open the door to offsets for genetically modified crops and large-scale biochar land grabs, which would be a disaster for Africa. Africa is already suffering from a land grab epidemic – the race to control soils for carbon trading could only make this worse." "The voluntary soil carbon market will be just another space for financial speculation, and while farmers receive pennies, speculators will make any real profits. This is just another way for polluting industries and countries to evade real reductions in emissions. If we as farmers sign a soil carbon agreement we lose autonomy and control over our farming systems. Some bureaucrat on the other side of the world, who knows nothing about our soil, rainfall, slope, local food systems, family economy, etc., will decide what practices we should use or not use. It is inseparable from the neoliberal trend to convert absolutely everything (land, air, biodiversity, culture, genes, carbon, etc.) into capital, which in turn can be placed in some kind of speculative market."

According to the International Institute for Sustainable Development, "Forests cover some 635 million hectares in Africa, accounting for 16 per cent of the world's forests. Over 70 per cent of Africa's population depends on forests." Given the central importance of forests to Africa's wellbeing, it is urgent that more comprehensive research be done on the implications of REDD for the vast majority of the population. Although the *No REDD in Africa Network* database has data from only a sampling of 118 projects from 23 countries, it is possible to begin to detect some important trends.

The NRAN database identified the following types of REDD-type projects in Africa: forest carbon, afforestation and reforestation (with native or exotic trees), monoculture tree plantations, official REDD, Blue Carbon or Wet Carbon (for example in wetlands or mangroves), Climate Smart Agriculture (for example, with farming, fruit or nut trees, fuel wood, soil carbon, biochar), Gourmet REDD, Clean Development Mechanism (CDM) projects, PES (Payment for Environmental Services), jatropha plantations (possibly for agrofuels), biomass, fair trade frameworks and feasibility studies, among others.

Land tenure arrangements of the projects in the database include collective community or private land tenure, protected areas, national parks, regional biospheres, multinational conservation areas and biological corridors. Projects are being done in a diversity of land and water ecosystems including forests, mangroves, wetlands, farms, orchards, coasts, plantations and arid areas. Project scale varies from small plots to very large regional initiatives. It is noteworthy that a number of the projects use sophisticated surveillance technology and remote sensors. Satellite technology is also probably used for carbon inventory and accounting. Funding for the projects tends to be from private and foreign bilateral or multilateral sources.

7. REDD players in Africa

The following is by no means a complete list of each sector active on REDD in Africa, but it is a start. Promoters of REDD in Africa include many of the corporations and UN agencies shown in the graphic *Who benefits from REDD? Players and Power*. REDD players in Africa identified in the database include the following: (There is some overlap between funders, carbon traders and NGOs.)

Countries and Regional Bodies

African countries and ministries of the environment, agriculture, forests, tourism, nature, mines; national forest and parks authorities; Norway, European Union, United States, European Space Agency (ESA) and OSFAC (satellite observatory for central African forests) and BRICS among others. BRICS is an acronym for an association of five major emerging national economies, which is considered "sub-imperial" by some observers: Brazil, Russia, India, China, and South Africa. BRICS members are promoting REDD.

REDD is not just being developed nationally, regional initiatives are also afoot. According to the South African Development Community (SADC) REDD+ Information Network, during the SADC Ministerial Meeting that took place in Windhoek, Namibia on 26th May 2011, the SADC Ministers including Mozambique approved a regional REDD+ Programme for Southern Africa. The SADC Support Programme on REDD provides a comprehensive framework for the region to actively participate in and benefit from the carbon market. The programme's purpose is to "contribute to strengthening capacities in the Member States to design REDD policies and programmes while at the same time providing a framework for strategic cooperation among Member States on issues of regional interest." The programme document on *SADC Support Programme on Reducing Emission from Deforestation and Forest Degradation (REDD+)* was approved by the Ministers responsible for Environment and Natural Resources Management.

It is probable that Mozambique is serving as a laboratory for REDD pilot projects that will be subsequently replicated both by SADC and others in Southern Africa as a region, as well as in Africa as a continent. In this regard the status of land grabs in Mozambique is relevant as the emerging Mozambican pattern of REDD and land grabs may be applied in other African countries. These trends are being resisted by peoples in the region. The Congo Basin Forest Fund is also promoting regional REDD coordination.

UN Agencies, Banks and Funders

World Bank, Global Environmental Facility (GEF) World Bank Forest Carbon Partnership Facility, World Bank BioCarbon Fund, African Development Bank, United Nations Environment Program (UNEP), UN-REDD, IUCN (International Union for the Conservation of Nature), Congo Basin Forest Fund (CBFF), with funding from the European Union, Norway and others; KfW Bankengruppe, Department for International Development (United Kingdom), Spain-UNEP partnership for Protected Areas, Danish International Development Agency (Danida), Department for International Development – UK, Government of Germany, USAID, AFD/FEM - public French donors, Nedbank, and German Technical Corp, among others.

NGOs, Institutes and Churches

WWF, Conservation International, World Resources Institute (WRI), Wildlife Conservation Society (WCS), GTZ, CARE International, Global Witness, Green Belt Movement, REDDAF – REDD in Africa, Code REDD, Envirotrade, Planet Action, Ethiopian Wetlands and Natural Resource Association (EWNRA), BCI – The Bonobo Conservation Initiative, Zoological Society of London, CED (Centre for Environment and Development), NOVATEL, Planet Survey (formerly SNV), GFA Envest, Treedom, Nature Plus, Sangha Trinational Park grant making programme, GAF AG, Alternatives to Slassh-and-Burn Partnership, Jadora, Capno International Developments, Joint Organization of Ecologists and Friends of Nature (OCEAN), Livelihood Venture, Archdiocese of Kikwit, BioCarbon Partners, ECOTRUST, Achats Services International (ASI), The Clinton Hunter Development Initiative, Malawi Environmental Trust (MEET), TBC, Vi Agroforestry (ViA), Wildlife Works, Inc., Tree Flights, Tany Meya Foundation, The Holistic Conversation

Programme for Forests (HCPF), Institute for the Conservation of Tropical Environments (ICTE), Bioclimate, Oceanium, Wildlands, Conservation Trust, International Small Group and Tree Planting Program, Face the Future (formerly FACE), Nature Office, VI Agroforestry, Mpingo Conservation & Development Initiative, World Vision Australia, World Vision Ethiopia, A Rocha Ghana, FORM, Eco2librium, Sustainable Use of Biomass - SUB//global-woods, Carbon Green Investments Guernsey Ltd., Sable Transport, Ltd - land owner, Etc Terra, Clean Air Corporation, Camco, Fan Bolivia, GFW, Cameroon Institute of Oceanographic and Fisheries Research, Center for Tropical Research (CTR), Climate Stewards (UK), Community Forest Associations, Coordination Nationale, Ecosur Afrique and PrimaKlima-Weltweit, pension funds among others.

Universities
Arlomom Senegal (Cheikh Anta Diop University of Dakar), State University of New York Stony Brook, University of Edinburgh and the Edinburgh Centre for Carbon Management, among others.

Companies
Shell Trading, Forest Stewardship Council, Disney Productions, GMbH, Safbois SPRL - logging company, affiliate of American Trading Company, and «forest company» Pallisco, among others.

Carbon Traders
Global Green Carbon Corp, Carbon Me, South Pole Carbon Asset Management Ltd., Carbon Tanzania, Envirotrade Carbon Limited, ERA Carbon Offsets Canada (clients include Shell Canada and lululemon athletica), Catalyst Paper, Harbour, HSE-Entega, Vancity, Almia, Carbon Offset and Carbon2Green Development, Ltd, among others.

Certifiers:

Voluntary Carbon Standard; Climate, Community and Biodiversity (CCB); CDM; TUV-SUD (CDM Validation); JACO (CDM Validation); Det Norske Veritas; Scientific Certification Systems (SCS); CarbonFix; American Carbon Registry; Rainforest Alliance Standard: Plan Vivo; World Bank BioCarbon Fund Standard; Ernst & Young; Environmental Services, Inc. (ESI), among others.

Buyers of African forest carbon or other carbon credits

These include, but are by no means limited to: the State of California, Canada (IBRD), Canada (Carbon2Green), World Bank BioCarbon Fund, IUCN (International Union for Conservation of Nature), Italy and Italy (BioCarbon), among others.

8. The carbon market: Selling African air

> *We fear for the air around us.*
> *Fela Kuti*

The global carbon market is estimated to eventually generate 1-3 trillion dollars a year.[27] In 2010, it was estimated to be at $120.9 billion.[28] Some have even speculated that carbon credits could eventually replace the US dollar as the new global currency.[29] Even the World Bank does not think the idea is that far-fetched: "You can imagine a future world where carbon is really the currency of the 21st century."[30]

Two African carbon "stock markets" are already buying and selling "Made in Africa" carbon offsets: the African Carbon Exchange (ACX)"[31] in Kenya and the African Carbon Credit Exchange (ACCE)[32] in Zambia. These exchanges hope to profit from carbon offsets generated in Africa,[33] be they under the Clean Development Mechanism (CDM) or REDD. At the UNFCCC COP17 in December 2011, there was no political will to create a second commitment period for the Kyoto Protocol, the only existing mandatory legally binding framework for greenhouse gas emissions reductions (though fundamentally flawed by major loopholes and the inclusion of carbon trading). However, COP17 does allow for the continuation and even expansion of the Clean Development Mechanism, a carbon trading mechanism that essentially outsources the industrialized countries' obligation to reduce emissions at source, to the Global South. So COP17 preserved the shell of the Kyoto Protocol devoid of commitments for GHG reductions targets, to increase the CDM, many of whose projects have already caused human rights violations and environmental destruction.[34]

In addition to the African carbon exchange and the African Carbon Credit Exchange, there is an annual trade fair for selling African air called the African

Carbon Forum,[35] which the United Nations Environment Program (UNEP) supports.[36] There are also plans to create an exchange in Senegal exclusively for African REDD credits. The Anglo African Energy Group, notorious for its environmental destruction, "is looking to develop a Senegal-based exchange where the forestry offsets can be traded."[37] Climate criminals like Shell Oil, which caused ecocide in Ogoniland in the Niger Delta, are already buying African air. In 2014, Reuters reported that Shell Trading was buying African carbon credits from Burundi and Uganda offered by Ecosur Afrique, which says it has 20 CDM projects registered in sub-Saharan Africa, making it the region's largest developer.[38]

Industrialized countries could find it easy to fulfill much of their targets for emissions reductions with cheap REDD offset credits.[39] According to *The Economist*, REDD "will push down the price. Companies would then buy cheap credits and continue doing business as usual rather than cutting their own emissions."[40] It's just "trading thin air."[41] Industrialized countries could offset most of their emissions with REDD thus not only not reducing climate change but making it worse and in the process "cooking the continent"[42] and resulting in the continuous incineration of Africa.[43] Even pro-REDD authors, who are eager for Africa to get more carbon funds, note that REDD could fuel conflict and harm peasants and indigenous peoples in Africa as the *No REDD in Africa Network* has documented. According to *Challenges and Prospects for REDD+ in Africa*, "there is a fear that a group of actors will exert its influence on REDD revenues to the detriment of vulnerable communities… REDD could then exacerbate conflicts over ownership and access to forest resources."[44]

REDD's Skyrocketing Scope

The World Bank is promoting a carbon credits project in Kenya with 60,000 small-scale farmers to reduce pesticide use, encourage sustainable agricultural practices and sell the resulting carbon credits. According to the *Global Alliance against REDD,* REDD could result in a counter-agrarian reform.[45] The implications of Climate Smart Agriculture for peasants and food sovereignty include the expropriation not just of land, but the commodification, perversion, privatization and patenting of entire sustainable and organic agricultural knowledge systems.[46] It is also a way to divert attention from the massive carbon emissions produced by industrial farming and agribusiness, especially in the North, and place the burden of reducing emissions on peasants in the South.[47]

Climate Smart Agriculture could be particularly bad for women who grow as much as 80% of food in some African countries. The land grabs and evictions that REDD may cause could make it particularly difficult for women to feed their families, In addition, since women rarely have the title to the land they till, it is difficult for them to contest land grabs. The Assembly of Rural Women of Southern Africa wasted no time in condemning REDD and the use of soils as carbon sinks.[48] Furthermore, "the aim to expand carbon markets onto African soil is thus about shifting the blame and responsibility for addressing climate change from rich countries onto African farmers, even though they are not the ones who have caused it."[49]

9. REDD as a driver of land grabs in Africa

Land grabs are rampant in Africa. Professor Patrick Mugo Mugo, a research associate in food security and community development, blames "the land rush on the increasing demand to acquire fertile land by a corporate global minority seeking bio-fuel crops and the new frontier; the need for carbon credits [which] has now turned into a lucrative business."[50] Other experts are warning that "three-quarters of Africa's population and two-thirds of its land are at risk."[51] In Africa, land grabs hinder sustainable development, Rights and Resources International notes that:

> Of the 203 million hectares of land deals reported worldwide between 2000 and 2010, two-thirds were in Africa. The acquisitions are dispossessing millions of Africans of their land, to make way for expansive forestry and mineral projects and plantations... But international efforts at sustainable development are also threatening these areas. Biofuels are made from crops that are often planted on former forest or marsh land, and carbon-offset projects can result in the eviction of inhabitants of wooded areas that are bought up in exchange for carbon credits... [T]he voluntary carbon market is... dispossessing local custodians of their lands. For example, Green Resources, a forestry company based in Oslo, has bought up hundreds of thousands of hectares of forests in Mozambique, threatening the food security and livelihoods of local populations by denying them access to their traditional lands and food sources. The company has also expanded to Uganda, Tanzania and southern Sudan. A Dutch firm's carbon-offset project in Uganda's Mount Elgon National Park became unmarketable after sustained conflict with local farmers who contest the group's right to the land.[52]

There is a direct corollary between land grabbing in Africa and emerging climate policy based on offsets in Northern countries and at the UN. Even a carbon trader publication like *Point Carbon* acknowledged that: "The mere prospect of deforestation credits being recognized in a new US climate bill has been enough to spark a REDD land grab in Central Africa."[53]

To understand how REDD is emerging as a significant driver of past and present massive land grabs in Africa, it is useful to identify two distinct phases of land grabbing. In the first phase, land was grabbed mostly for plantations, export crops and agrofuels. In the second phase, land was grabbed for these purposes as well as for carbon credits and REDD. But since REDD's scope has expanded to include plantations, soils, agriculture and all landscapes and ecosystems, all the land grabbed in the first phase can also now become REDD projects. For example, in Mozambique, "[e]xisting large-scale plantations in Niassa and Nampula are also taking advantage of REDD+ and the Clean Development Mechanism, by seeking to certify the plantations as carbon sinks, thus generating more profit for the investors."[54]

Furthermore, there are financial, political and legal incentives to do so because if a tree plantation or an export flower farm or a jatropha agrofuel operation gets REDD credits, it adds an additional source of income, subsidies, legal recognition and certification, and can even cloak itself in the legitimacy of supposedly saving the climate.

First phase of land grabs
- Plantations
- Monocultures agricultural export crops
- Agrofuels

Second phase of land grabs
- Plantations, export crops and agrofuels
- Conversion of first phase grabs into REDD projects
- REDD (all landscapes and ecosystems)
- REDD-ification of Africa and the Continent Grab for Carbon Colonialism

Thus, REDD simultaneously reinforces past land grabs by making them more profitable, legal and legitimate; drives land grabs for carbon credits in and of themselves; and drives new land grabs for these other activities that are "REDD-able" as well. Vast tracts of Africa are also being labeled "unused"and "degraded" to justify land grabbing. In Tanzania, for example, "the draft National REDD strategy justifies the classification of 49 % of forests as being on general land by stating that, 'General Land as used here means all public land which is not reserved or village land including unoccupied or unused village land.' On the same page, the strategy also states, 'Forests in General Land are 'open access', characterized by unsecured land tenure, shifting cultivation, annual wild fires, harvesting of wood fuel, poles and timber, and heavy pressure for conversion to other competing land uses, such as agriculture, livestock grazing, settlements and industrial development.' Confusingly, in these two definitions, land that communities use for agriculture, harvesting of wood products, grazing and even settlement is defined as 'unused'."[55]

The Ecologist reports that the lack of forest definition is a 'major obstacle' in the fight to protect rainforests: "ambiguous forest definitions are putting the future success of forest protection schemes in doubt and allowing logging companies to destroy biodiverse habitats. The current lack of a working definition of what degraded forest or land is 'plays into the hands' of logging companies, say forest campaigners. The companies claim to responsibly develop 'only on degraded land', but in reality this can actually mean they are clearing forests and peatlands."[56]

According to Isilda Nhantumbo, a Mozambican expert at the pro-REDD International Institute for Environment and Development and former consultant with the World Bank, REDD may create generations of landless people. "REDD+ is now driving a race for land in Mozambique...British capital wants to 'invest' in REDD+ projects. The total area identified is 150,000 km2, equivalent to 15 million ha or 19% of the country's surface. The selection of areas for this private 'investment' was based on the proposed

REDD+ pilots". Ms. Nhamtumbo asks: "Am I witnessing the creation of generations of landless people in Mozambique and Africa in general?"[57]

It is a question worth asking. Carbon trading companies have applied for rights to one-third of Mozambique, to sell REDD credits.[58] More than 40% of Cameroon's forests – almost 20% of the country – may be slated for REDD-type projects.[59] In Liberia, 20% forests were almost grabbed for a billionaire carbon scam.[60] According to Reuters, an Australian carbon trading company claimed to have signed a contract to do REDD in all of the 2,345,000 square kilometers of the entire national territory of Democratic Republic of Congo,[61] which was subsequently declared illegal. This incident serves to illustrate the dishonesty and ambition of some carbon traders.[62] These percentages while staggering, may be just the tip of the REDD iceberg given the lack of disclosure which is typical of such dealings. The actual amount of land being grabbed for carbon trading may be much greater.

10. Climate smart agriculture is dumb!

Landscape REDD includes fields, farms, forests and Climate Smart Agriculture. Climate Smart Agriculture generates carbon credits from fossil fuel-dependent agro-business, "climate ready crops," GMOs, agrofuels, sugar and soybean plantations and other destructive agricultural practices.

According to Doreen Stabinsky, a professor of global environmental politics, "'Climate Smart Agriculture' is a feeble attempt to green the image of industrial agriculture – a difficult task given that fertilizer production and use and industrial beef production emit huge quantities of greenhouse gases. Over 100 civil society and farmers organizations from around the world are loudly rejecting a new US initiative, the Global Alliance on Climate-smart Agriculture."[63]

According to La Via Campesina, the world's largest peasant movement, "soil carbon markets could also open the door to offsets for genetically modified crops and large-scale land grabs for biochar." Biochar is charcoal used as a soil amendment. Like most charcoal, it is made from biomass via pyrolysis. It is promoted by some as an approach to carbon sequestration. However, vast monocultures of fast-growing tree plantations would be needed to provide the necessary raw material if biochar carbon sequestration were to be implemented on a large scale. Peter Reed, an energy lecturer in New Zealand, coined the word biochar in 2005. He reckons that an area of 1.4 billion hectares should be enough. That's a little more than the total area of arable land in the world! Africa is already suffering from a land grab epidemic – the race to control soils for carbon trading and sequestration could only make this worse.

In May 2009, the Congo Basin Forest Fund announced the first and so far only REDD-related grant for the use of biochar, i.e. fine-grained charcoal added to agricultural soils. The €338,000 grant went towards a project in the Democratic Republic of Congo called "Phasing out Slash-and-Burn farming with Bio-char". The project was initiated by a Belgian-based 'social profit organisation' called Biochar Fund, together with a local partner organisation, ADAPEL. According to the Congo Basin Forest Fund's (CBFF) website, the project will "replace slash-and-burn farming" because biochar 'maintains soil fertility and constitutes a stable and easily measurable carbon sink. Bio-char thus enriches the soil and makes it more productive, which lessens the pressure to encroach on forest land. Using crop residues to produce bio-char also generates renewable energy in a low-cost manner, and this reduces local dependency on firewood.' None of those claims have been borne out by scientific field trials…The CBFF biochar grant was not only a 'first' as far as biochar funding is concerned – it is also the only CBFF grant to support a technology or practice claimed to sequester carbon in soils. Carbon credits for soil carbon sequestration are one of the aims pursued by the World Bank in Durban and beyond.

"The voluntary soil carbon market will be another space for financial speculation, and while farmers receive pennies, speculators will make ridiculous profits. This is just another way for polluting industries and countries to evade real reductions in emissions. If we as farmers sign a soil carbon agreement, we lose autonomy and control over our farming systems. It is inseparable from the neoliberal ideology of converting absolutely everything (land, air, biodiversity, culture, genes, carbon, etc.) into capital, which in turn can be placed in some kind of speculative market."[64]

A new form of colonialism

The *No REDD in Africa Network* has, since its creation, declared categorically that "REDD is not just a false solution to climate change but is emerging as a new form of colonialism, economic subjugation, impoverishment and land grabs so massive that they may constitute a Continent Grab."[65] Many social movements, academics and analysts agree.

In the "NO REDD+! in RIO+20 – A Declaration to Decolonize the Earth and the Sky," the Global Alliance against REDD+ did not mince words:

"After more than 500 years of resistance, we, Indigenous Peoples, local communities, peasant farmers, fisherfolk and civil society are not fooled by the so-called Green Economy and REDD+ because we know colonialism when we see it. Regardless of its cynical disguises and shameful lies, colonialism always results in the rape and pillaging of Mother Earth, and the slavery, death, destruction and genocide of her peoples."[66]

Kathleen McAfee, author of "The Contradictory Logic of Global Ecosystem Services Markets," concurs that market-based conservation efforts will repeat the historic pattern of colonialist pillaging by extracting wealth from the rural Global South and concentrating it in Northern financial hubs. "Application in international conservation policy of the market model, in which profit incentives depend upon differential opportunity costs, will entail a net upward redistribution of wealth from poorer to wealthier classes and from rural regions to distant centers of capital accumulation, mainly in the global North."[67]

Insights about capital accumulation from nature and carbon sequestration in Africa can be garnered from Sarah Bracking's, "How do Investors Value Environmental Harm/Care? Private Equity Funds, Development Finance Institutions and the Partial Financialization of Nature-based Industries?"

"Private equity funds, mostly domiciled in secrecy jurisdictions, are dominant investors in the resource-based economies of Africa. Some of the investments that these funds make have been speculative and based on perceived high-value 'futures' in biodiversity, bio-fuels and land, carbon capture or strategic minerals. However, private equity funds are also heavily invested in mining, energy and infrastructure, which also generate wealth from the non-human world; 'old' markets alongside the 'new' markets for discovered nature-based commodities...[T]hese calculative devices assist in legitimizing private equity funds as institutional leaders in pre-existing power structures which exploit natural resources in Africa for the benefit of money-holders. These propositions roughly correspond to the technical, empirical and theoretical dimensions of a socio-technical arrangement applying to nature-based accumulation, which, overall, performs a political process of financialization."[68]

11. Blue carbon and wet carbon

REDD projects are also being carried out in mangroves, wetlands, oceans and marine protected areas. The United Nations Environment Program's Blue Carbon Initiative is quick to point out that the ocean stores about 93% of the planet's carbon dioxide[69] and should be included in carbon trading. "Blue carbon" refers to the use of plankton, sea grasses, algae and mangroves of the ocean as carbon sinks to generate carbon credits through carbon sequestration.

"Wet carbon" refers to a similar treatment of wetlands. In 2009, according to the WWF the Danone Fund for Nature, a partnership of the Danone Group, IUCN and Ramsar, "launched an initiative to finance projects that preserve and restore wetlands – so-called wet carbon – to offset the carbon emissions of some of Danone's brands (e.g. Evian). The fund has already supported a first pilot project for mangrove planting in Senegal. So a company that privatizes and bottles drinking water is also privatizing water ecosystems. WWF also has its eye on Mozambique's beautiful coasts as carbon sinks and for using REDD and carbon markets to finance protected areas and national parks in conjunction with the sale of other environmental services.[70] *Blue Carbon: The Opportunity of Coastal Sinks for Africa* shows that all of Africa, whether land or sea or water may be used as a sponge for emissions.[71]

Any strategy to protect Africa from REDD and false solutions to climate change should monitor various carbon sequestration schemes such as plans to do Carbon Capture and Storage (CCS) which might include trying to pump CO_2 into the bottom of the ocean or into the ground. It is crucial to note that Blue Carbon and Wet Carbon are undoubtedly linked to water grabs and water privatization. In fact, increasingly analysts are asking if African land grabs are not really covers for water grabs. The following discussion of Gourmet REDD addresses these overlapping grabs and cites the example of Gourmet REDD in the Lake Niassa area.

Blue Grabbing in Africa

Mary Galvin

http://canadians.org/blog/blue-grabbing-africa

The wave of land grabs over the last few years has been at a massive scale. These large scale land acquisitions have serious implications for agriculture, ecology, and agrarian change. People are dispossessed and often dislocated, and employment is adversely affected.

Since 2011, over 45 million hectares have been grabbed in Africa (a conservative estimate by the World Bank). Aims include mining, forestry, agri-business, biofuels, and conservation/ tourism, although in Africa the main aim of large grabbers like China and India is agricultural. Again, this paints a picture of BRICS (Brazil, Russia, China, India and South Africa) as driving a new scramble for Africa. Financial, food and energy crises are resulting in pressures to find profitable avenues for finance, to produce food for growing countries like China and India, and to produce energy through biofuels. And water is the key element in each of these areas.

In a context where land rights are not formalised and population growth means there is competition for scarce resources, there is scope for the World Bank and IMF to present land acquisition (grabs) as a «development opportunity» and many African governments respond positively. They are pleased to get funds for investment, so they offer cheap land with 99-year leaseholds, and provide tax exemptions. Information on these deals in being compiled through a range of sources into a land matrix, which can give insights but does not include many formalized deals in progress or emerging through local entities. According to this matrix, Mozambique and Ethiopia are currently the African countries with the largest number of deals and hectares grabbed. Even in Uganda, where foreign acquisitions of land are illegal since the expulsion of Asian people in 1969, 13 per cent of agricultural land has been grabbed by using leasehold and local legal entities that are owned by Indian capital. Countries such as Zambia have now put ceilings on land acquisitions.

In contrast, South Africa's agribusiness operates as a sub-imperial power, supported by Pretoria in its role as one of the BRICS. South Africa's AgriSA signed the largest single African deal of 10 million hectares, approximately twice the size of Switzerland, although only 200,000 hectares have been used so far for agricultural production. So South Africa is a significant player alongside Egypt and Libya, moving away from the typical logic of Northern grabs from the Southern countries. The scope for this deal was created by the South African government signing bilateral agreements with a range of African countries. South African agri-business companies, supported by Pretoria, have 27 registered land deals in Southern and Eastern Africa.

One of the main areas of South African grabbing is related to its growing sugar industry, in which Illovo Sugar is the main player (SADC, the Southern African Development Community, is among the top 15 global producers). Sugar is produced to meet growing national consumption, with the market expanding by an average of two per cent per year in African countries. But bio-mass is also used to produce ethanol, supporting the renewable energy targets of the European Union.

Sugar Factories in Southern Africa

«Blue grabs» or water grabs are a serious--yet typically overlooked-- part of land grabs. They raise the central issue of water ownership. Water use is a stunning omission from the land acquisition (grab) contracts, but the inclusion of water use would certainly undermine the plausibility of these «development opportunities». For example, almost all sugar estates draw their water from rivers for irrigation, to the detriment of small scale farmers that rely on the same rivers for water. Moreover the sugar mills consume enormous amounts of water. In Mali the course of the Niger has been diverted via the construction of an artificial canal to serve a project called Malibya that involved 100.000 hectares to produce wet rice then exported back to Libya. It transformed arid savannah into Vietnam-style rice plantations (see

Martiniello, G. «Dispossession and rural social movements: the 2011 Conference in Mali», Review of African Political Economy).

Without a mass mobilisation of citizenry against country's elites, land and water grabs will devastate the poor populations of countries in the same way that enclosures did in England in the 18th and 19th century. This wave of land grabs is leading to mass dispossession, displacement, adverse incorporation of outgrowers and increasing indebtedness, land concentration, and agri-business transnationalism. Activist-academics are working closely with communities to establish the history of areas that are being dispossessed, so that they can contest these new «enclosures» in court. Together with social justice activists, they are raising awareness that supports the mobilisation by local populations against land and water grabs and their devastating impact on livelihoods.

12. Gourmet REDD

One way for capitalists to increase their profit margin and create new forms of rent is to add aggregate value to their products. Gourmet REDD adds layers of additional values to carbon credits and makes them more profitable and marketable because of their fancy, exotic allure to consumers in industrialized countries.

For example, REDD credits from Mozambican oceans and mangroves could be combined with biodiversity offsets and the protection of butterflies, endemic starfish and community marine resource management, including the protection of whale sharks. The key reference material for understanding Gourmet REDD is in the report, *Cashing in on Creation: Gourmet REDD privatizes, packages, patents, sells and corrupts all that is Sacred.* [72]

The Gourmet REDD Recipe looks like this:

REDD

\+ Payment for Environmental Services

\+ Biodiversity Offsets

\+ Water Offsets

\+ "Sustainable Development"

\+ Traditional Cultures

= Compounded Commodification or

Privatization of Air, Life & Culture

Gourmet REDD is a combination of REDD and other kinds of offsets. To sugar-coat REDD and greenwash pollution with ploys like Climate Change Chocolate,[73] there are norms, standards, third-party verifiers, certification systems,[74] "small-scale, cute and cuddly carbon projects," and "the gourmet niche of the carbon market."[75] Another way to dress up carbon trading[76] and make even more money is to combine REDD with exotic forms of supposed compensation for environmental destruction. In these early years of the 21st century, everything is being turned into an environmental service or "offset". Selling Life to the highest bidder is all the rage.

Cooking up Gourmet REDD in Lake Niassa National Reserve? – WWF, Coca-Cola and USAID

The 4.2 million hectare Lake Niassa National Reserve looks like an excellent example of mega Gourmet REDD with an entire ecosystem in the making. Participants in this project include USAID, the Coca-Cola Company and WWF as well as the Ministries of Tourism, Fisheries, Environment and Defense of Mozambique and the Niassa Provincial Government. Community "rangers" are "cooperating with the Navy to enforce existing laws surrounding illegal fishing, timber cutting, illegal migration, mining and piracy."[77] This makes it sounds like they are getting ready to "police" the Gourmet REDD project.

WWF, whose green mask was recently ripped off in the report, *Panda Leaks: The Dark Side of WWF,*[78] has already conducted "pre-feasibility work for biochar in the proposed Lake Niassa reserve and is exploring the potential for forest carbon in other sites."[79] Biochar requires large quantities of timber from plantations which is then burned and buried as this is supposed to sequester carbon, a claim that has been heavily criticized and de-bunked by various environmental groups. (REDD biochar has also been piloted in the Democratic Republic of Congo and Cameroon[80] with support from the Congo Basin Forest Fund.[81])

Coca-Cola may be participating in the Lake Niassa REDD proposal given its interest in controlling and privatizing sources of fresh water, as it has done in India.[82] In fact, Coca-Cola's bottled water business could eventually eclipse the success of its teeth-rotting soft drink given the spiraling world water crisis, the global momentum of water privatization, and access to water as a subtext of armed conflict and war.

Coca-Cola is clearly aware that Lake Niassa is the second largest lake in Africa and a key hydric resource for Malawi and Mozambique. The availability of water including the annual rainfall is also a part of Mozambique's attractiveness as a host for REDD pilot projects for Africa,. Without a doubt, land grabs and water grabs go hand in hand, and Lake Niassa may be a perfect example of just that.

The United States Agency for International Development (USAID) is Mozambique's largest bilateral donor. USAID supports the Gorongosa National Park and the creation of Lake Niassa Reserve. Through the Northern Mozambique Tourism Project, USAID supports nature-based tourism. USAID has expressed interest in developing innovative carbon projects and public-private partnerships."[83]

According to Carbon Plus Capital – Biocarbon Finance,[84] "The Ministry of Coordination of Environmental Affairs (MICOA) of the Government of Mozambique is responsible for the development of a national REDD-plus strategy. As part of this strategy, MICOA is working with Carbon-Plus Capital on a pioneering conservation financing mechanism based on aligning the interests of conservation, sustainable development and climate change mitigation with those of private capitale. Focused on the country's unique 4.2 million hectare Niassa National Reserve, the project is being developed as a model of forestry-based carbon management to inform and inspire the evolution of an effective REDD-plus system globally."[85]

13. Funding for REDD in Africa

According to the World Bank, "The Africa Carbon Forum 2011, held in Marrakesh, Morocco, saw more than 1,000 participants exploring new carbon finance opportunities in Africa."[86] By 2011, more than 7.7 billion dollars had already been committed (but not necessarily actually delivered) for REDD by donor countries,[87] and more than $35 million a year for REDD is being dished out by global foundations.[88] Other funding sources for REDD includes UN-REDD, UNEP, World Bank and its diverse carbon project programs. It is difficult to ascertain what percentage of these funds goes to Africa since the voluntary and mandatory markets do not compile such data. Funding for REDD in Africa includes $22.3 million disbursed from UN-REDD to five African countries that have national programs, namely the (Congo, DRC, Nigeria, Tanzania and Zambia). In 2013, the Congo Basin Forest Fund, many of whose projects are REDD, aspired to disburse 17 million Euros.[89]

The following chart show Voluntary REDD Funding as reported by funders, which may overlap with the amount from the Congo Basin Forest Fund to some degree. The amounts for each country presented online in the Voluntary REDD Funding map have been registered and tallied in the accompanying Voluntary REDD Chart. The total amount of voluntary REDD Funding for more than 40 African countries is $1.192 billion. The $198.68 million for the Democratic Republic of Congo is the highest amount followed by $135.12 million for Tanzania, where there have been scandals about the REDD corruption and conflicts; [90] and $55.16 million for Mozambique. It is also interesting that so many arid countries are funded, which may point to landscape REDD including carbon sequestration from deserts.

Country	Voluntary REDD Funding (millions of dollars)
Angola	0.45
Algeria	0.63
Benin	24.14
Botswana	0.47
Burkina Faso	94.28
Cameroon	48.51
Central African Republic	36.26
Chad	13.58
Congo	23.26
Cote d'Ivoire	45.48
DRC	198.68
Ethiopia	51.94
Equatorial Guinea	6.03
Gabon	28.18
Ghana	90.96
Guinea	0.8
Guinea Bissau	1.6
Kenya	35.18
Liberia	26.76
Niger	10.1
Nigeria	24.43
Madagascar	13.6
Malawi	36.13
Mali	32.08
Mauritania	9.07
Morocco	28.9
Mozambique	55.16
Namibia	0.76

Rwanda	27.11
Senegal	19.04
São Tomé and Principe	6.05
Sierra Leone	8.31
South Africa	0.32
Sudan	4.1
Uganda	8.83
Tanzania	135.12
Togo	4.79
Tunisia	12.73
Zambia	28.68
Zimbabwe	5.8
TOTAL	1.1925 billion dollars

Source: http://www.fao.org/forestry/vrd/

As the following graphic of the *Regional Distribution of Voluntary REDD Funding* shows, Africa has received less voluntary funding than Asia or Latin America. The voluntary funding from domestic sources for Latin American REDD is significant, while Asia and Africa have none. The lesser sum received by Africa does not necessarily mean that REDD in Africa is implemented in a smaller landmass, since costs for doing REDD in Africa may be lower than the other regions.

Regional Distribution of Voluntary REDD Funding

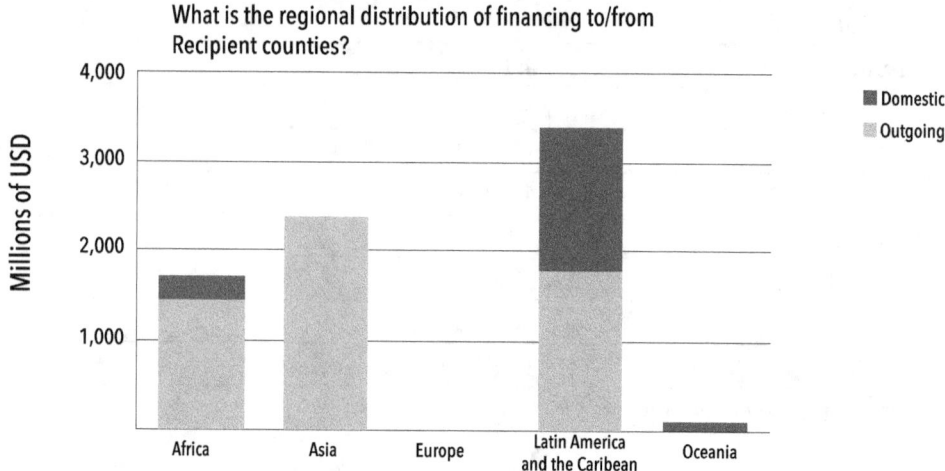

Total outgoing and domestic financial contibutions to recipient countries over time (2006-2018), as reported by funders.

Regional Distribution of Voluntary REDD Funding: Total outgoing and domestic financial contributions to recipient countries over time (2006-2018) as reported by funders. Source: http://www.fao.org/forestry/vrd/#graphs_and_stats

14. REDD and human rights violations

Human rights violations from REDD projects include a killing, criminalization of activists, violent evictions of tens of thousands of peoples, as well as threats to cultural survival and potential genocide, as the forced relocation of and "scorched earth" policy against the Sengwer People in Kenya shows. However, the impacts of REDD in Africa are not limited to violations of individual and collective human rights. REDD is firmly on course to further entrench existing systemic and structural oppressions related to access to and control over natural resources. REDD constitutes a new offensive against the people of Africa, especially those who are already marginalized (economically, politically, culturally) such as women, small-holder farmers, pastoralists, hunter gatherers and indigenous peoples.

The *No REDD in Africa Network* has documented and denounced the crucial emblematic case of the forced relocation and possible "extinction" of the Sengwer people as part of World Bank-funded REDD, which proves the genocidal potential of REDD. *The Guardian*'s Nafeez Ahmed reported on the "scorched earth campaign" in Cherangany Hills and how the "plight of Kenya's indigenous Sengwer shows carbon offsets are empowering corporate recolonisation of the South."[91] The evictions of the Sengwer also confirm Friends of the Earth International's concern that REDD could "foster an 'armed protection' mentality that could lead to the displacement of millions of forest-dependent people, through the police and military forces."[92]

Chris Lang of REDD Monitor notes that under REDD schemes, "the rights to the use of that land could be taken away from indigenous peoples who depend on their forests for their livelihoods. Destroying livelihoods on this scale could conform to the parts (a), (b), and (c) of the definition of genocide [of the United Nations Convention on the Prevention of Genocide][93]."

Gravity of human rights violations and magnitude of the repression

It is important to note the scope, diversity and gravity of the human rights violations REDD-type projects are causing. The magnitude of the repression of REDD-type projects already includes the violent eviction of tens of thousands of people. The forest carbon project in Uganda for the New Forests Company is not an aberration, but rather indicative of the scale of repression and militarization that is possible under REDD-type projects.

REDD-type projects are violating not just the individual rights of persons but also the collective rights of peoples including the right to exist as a people, and the right to self-determination enshrined in Article 1 of the International Covenant on Civil and Political Rights and the International Covenant on Social, Economic and Cultural Rights; as well as article 3 of the United Nations Declaration on the Rights of Indigenous Peoples (UNDRIPs). The articles of UNDRIPs most commonly violated by REDD-type projects are found in Appendix 1.

The right to free, prior, informed consent is one of the fundamental principles of UNDRIPs and crucial for resisting the imposition of unwanted projects. A comparative analysis of the violation of the right to free, prior, informed consent by UN-REDD is revealing. Of the sixteen countries with UN-REDD national programs, at least ten countries have violated the right to free, prior and informed consent and the right to participate of civil society and indigenous peoples in processes related to REDD. (Appendix 2)

No mandatory safeguards

There are no legal binding safeguards pertaining to REDD and the REDD safeguards of the United Nations are not in the operative section of the document. They are rather left in an annex, voluntary and toothless.[94] No dispute mechanism has been established, let alone a grievance mechanism.

The UN's REDD safeguards neither save nor guard. The voluntary market as its name suggests is even more unregulated than the mandatory market.

Undoubtedly the number, intensity and magnitude of the human rights abuses will dramatically increase once REDD enters into its implementation phase. In this regard, the timeline for implementation suggests that REDD will start up in 2020, but there is a vocal coalition that is pushing for interim implementation before 2020. Furthermore, the "bankability" of credits allows polluters to amass and stockpile credits preemptively for upcoming mandatory reductions through offsets. The voluntary market and regional or subnational markets have their own timelines and some are already implementing REDD.

REDD causes systemic and structural changes

It is important to note that REDD is not just causing grave individual and collective human rights violations, it is causing systemic and structural changes. These changes touch almost every aspect of society including land, work, production, gender, immigration, power, independence, colonialism and, of course, global warming and the environment of the continent. Here is a compilation of these changes:

- Massive land grabs which could destroy traditional land and water tenure
- Changes in labor and work such as turning peasants and indigenous peoples into peons or carbon slaves in their own lands
- Changes in production
    - ◊ Growing carbon instead of food
    - ◊ Carbon capture instead of sustenance from forests
- A new form of violence against women
- An additional driver of immigration and exodus from countryside to cities and industrialized countries

- A new form of underdevelopment of Africa
- A new form of colonialism, economic subjugation and impoverishment
- A new form of capital accumulation, financialization and concentration of wealth
- Undermining nation states and increasing elite, corporate and foreign power
- Changes in legal framework especially of forests, land tenure and human rights
- Greater militarization, surveillance and control of forests, land, coasts and natural resources
- Less independence and more foreign intervention
- Redrawing of geopolitical maps
- Turn Africa into a carbon dump
- Continental conversion of native ecosystems to monoculture plantations
- Make global warming worse and contribute to the incineration of Africa

15. Labor and work: Peonage and carbon slavery

Relevant examples of how REDD could intensify exploitation of people and result in carbon slave-like conditions include: the Rio+20 model N'hambita REDD project in Mozambique whose contract binds peasants into multi-generational carbon slavery; the model World Bank Ibi-bateke Carbon Plantation where Batwa Pigmy may suffer servitude; and the evictions in Uganda that turned successful farmers into peons in their own land for the New Forests Company timber plantation. The extreme exploitation and inhumanity of these projects are not mistakes or exceptions but rather an integral and central part of the REDD strategy. As early as 2000, the International Forum of Indigenous Peoples and Local Communities on Climate Change in its first plenary statement to the United Nations prophetically vowed that "we do not want to be slaves of the carbon trade!"[95]

The tendency to maximize profits characterizes capitalism. Profits maximization often includes maximization of exploitation. This may shape the kind of labor required for REDD in Africa and the plantations of trees, agrofuels and crops. The carbon slavery and servitude of existing model REDD-type projects (i.e. N'hambita and Ibi-Bateke) indicate that carbon slavery may be a generalized feature of REDD in Africa.

The tendency of REDD to convert farmers and/or indigenous peoples into peons on their own land has already played out in the New Forest Company plantation in Uganda. Evicted successful farmers were reduced to becoming poorly paid plantation peons on the land they were evicted from. "Homeless and hopeless, Mr. Tushabe said he took a job with the company that pushed him out. He was promised more than $100 each month, he said, but received only about $30."[96]

The exploitation of the labor of local communities is facilitated by the extremely disadvantageous situations of evicted, homeless and dispossessed peoples with little or no recourse to legal support. This lack of recourse is compounded by the lack of interest of some in the international human rights community to denounce carbon trading. Except in a few isolated cases of human rights violations, most human rights NGOs limit themselves to seeking reform of the Clean Development Mechanism or to promoting safeguards.

With regard to changes in production, Landscape REDD and Climate Smart Agriculture pervert the task of growing food into growing carbon and may constitute a counter-agrarian reform. Much analysis remains to be done about how REDD in forest and water ecosystems changes production and affects labor. But one thing is clear: REDD is part of a new chapter in capitalism that could generate new forms of surplus value from nature and totally transform farmers' and forest dwellers' production systems, forms of work and exploitation, as well as relations of power associated with work.

16. REDD as a new form of violence against women

The *No REDD in Africa Network* and the *Global Alliance against REDD* have denounced REDD as a new form of violence against women in an Open Letter to the United Nations entitled *Carbon Trading, CDM and REDD: New Forms of Violence against Women NOT Women's Empowerment!*[97]

An excerpt follows:

> As women, we know that carbon trading and carbon offset projects violate our right to life because they increase pollution and make global warming worse. Carbon offset projects have resulted in land grabs, human rights abuses, violations of the rights of women, children, and Indigenous Peoples, forced displacement, armed guards, jailings, persecution and criminalization of activists. The carbon trading scam also means more asthma, heart disease and cancer for communities living near sources of pollution. Carbon markets cynically greenwash increased fossil fuel exploitation, extraction and combustion, which create toxic hot spots and toxic body burdens for women, affecting the right of future generations to a healthy life.

> As women who are guardians and collectors of water, we know that these false solutions allow polluting industries and governments to increase toxic emissions and releases, which poison our precious water. Furthermore, these false solutions to climate change cause more droughts, floods and natural disasters, during which women and children are 14 times more likely to die than men.[98]

> We celebrate Mother Earth and women. We reject carbon trading, the CDM and REDD, and denounce them as new forms of violence against women, children, local communities and Indigenous Peoples. We also reject the Women's Carbon Standard, 'gender sensitive carbon offset projects,' 'women and children methodologies' and the promotion and certification of carbon

trading and carbon offset projects of any kind, in terms of women's empowerment and leadership or our families' and children's wellbeing.

Pilot REDD-type projects in Africa are already negatively impacting women and children. Evicting some of the Ogiek People from the Mau Forest for UNEP-funded REDD, has hindered some Ogieks' traditional practices including hunting and gathering wild honey. According to Judy Kipkenda, Communications and Media Officer of the Ogiek Peoples Development Programme, some Ogiek women and girls are forced to prostitute themselves by the roadside where they are camped.[99] The studies of how REDD specifically affects women, girls and children; fuels gender violence and sexual exploitation as well as immigration from the forests and countryside are yet to be done, but all these forms of injustice are inherent to the scale of REDD land grabs.

****

As a carbon offset mechanism, REDD allows industrialized countries to use Africa's forests, agriculture, soils and even water ecosystems as sponges for their carbon dioxide pollution rather than cutting emissions at source. REDD allows the North to shirk its historical responsibilities as the main source of emissions and force the people of the South, those most affected by the climate crisis and least to blame for creating it, to carry this responsibility.[100]

However, offsets are really just the frosting on the REDD cake. Claiming to save the climate with REDD is a ploy for grabbing all the remaining land, water and energy in the world. In addition, according to Larry Lohmann, an expert on carbon trading, REDD also "creates new kinds of commodification and rent, provides new sources of profit for certain companies, pacifies and corrupts middle-class environmentalists, and creates new avenues for corporate theft from the state and the public."[101]

Furthermore, as REDD implementation advances, more REDD-type offset programs will include and actually promote fossil fuel extraction and mining in REDD project areas, as may happen in Ecuador's Socio Bosque.[102] It is highly probable that the REDD projects in Africa will do the same.

REDD with trees or even just grass is also planned as part of the expansion of mines, pipelines and other fossil fuel extraction, production and infrastructure sites. According to the president of the Chamber of Mines of the Philippines, Benjamin Phillip G. Romualdez, "the mining sector, and an extractive industry will need to replant trees in the vast tracts of lands in which they operate, hence, they might as well use the reforested trees as credits in the international carbon trade."[103] African mining consultant Steven Bluhm, CEO of Bluhm Burton Engineering (BBE) regrets that "South Africa is lagging behind in using the benefits that can be obtained from carbon credits."[104]

17. Financialization goes berserk: Offsetting the global supply chain and energy matrix

The takeover, commodification and privatization of nature by financial markets are known as the "financialization of nature."[105] According to Gerald Epstein "Financialisation means the increasing role of financial motives, financial markets, financial actors and financial institutions in the operation of the domestic and international economies."[106] Larry Lohmann explains financialization[107] as "super-commodification." "The drivers of the financialization of carbon and biodiversity assets [including REDD] are essentially the *same* as the drivers of financialization of any income-generating activity. The *difference* is that elsewhere it is fully-fledged commodities or well-established "fictitious commodities" such as land and labor that are being financialized, whereas carbon and biodiversity commodities have been created *during* the current era of financialization."

In the case of REDD, financialization includes the financial speculation on the hypothetical future behavior of stock generated from trading air.

"In general, it takes commodities that have been created through commensuration procedures and puts them through a further round of commensuration, putting them in the same pot with other commodities according to rates of return established in finance. They are further privatized, alienated, individuated, made abstract, revalued, displaced or liquefied in ways that allow them to earn quick rents more easily or serve as collateral for other things. From being entities whose value is realized when they face each other as commodities, they become entities whose value is realized when they confront each other as claims to the *future* value which supposedly will be produced in *future* activity and realized in *future* exchange."[108]

However, REDD goes beyond the financialization of air, forests and land and water and permits to pollute. As the New York Declaration on Forests announces, now REDD is moving towards "phasing out deforestation" and offsetting the entire global commodities supply chain. [109] REDD is not just a financialized commodity in and of itself but a financialized commodity ON TOP of the process of producing all commodities. Furthermore, REDD not only allows for the financialization of offsets, but also the financialization of the extraction, infrastructure and production of the energy from fossil fuels – the entire energy matrix – as well as the production of the components and manufacture of global commodities and chains, including third party suppliers. With REDD, financialization goes berserk. But unfortunately this is not just some carbon trader's fantasy; this is emerging international climate policy which is headed towards worldwide implementation. So the question is: How much of Africa does the UN, the US, Wall Street, Big Oil *et al* hope to grab?

Economic Subjugation and Impoverishment

Capital accumulation, financialization and financial speculation based on nature necessarily bring more economic subjugation. Our colleagues from Timberwatch are characteristically lucid in this regard: "If REDD-style schemes are allowed to be imposed on African forestland, fields and grasslands, it could mean the economic subjugation of the entire continent...REDD and CDM schemes will probably be no more than a form of re-colonisation, and the final drive to commodify the remaining spaces of Africa left in indigenous hands after the first round of formal colonialism."[110]

REDD will not benefit the poor and will result in greater impoverishment and misery. Even the REDD Policy Brief prepared by the Poverty Environment Partnership (PEP), whose member agencies include UNEP, UNDP and IUCN, is blunt in this regard. "REDD systems could present new risks for the poor" and "the poor may ultimately end up worse off." According to PEP, REDD could also result in "the concentration of power by elites."[111]

Kathleen McAfee agrees that REDD will be disastrous for the poor:

> Commodification and transnational trading of ecosystem services is the most ambitious iteration yet of the strategy of 'selling nature to save it'. The World Bank and UN agencies contend that global carbon markets can slow climate change while generating resources for development. Consonant with 'inclusionary' versions of neoliberal development policy, advocates assert that international payment for ecosystem services (PES) projects, financed by carbon-offset sales and biodiversity banking, can benefit the poor. However, the World Bank also warns that a focus on poverty reduction can undermine efficiency in conservation spending. The experience of ten years of PES illustrates how, in practice, market-efficiency criteria clash directly with poverty-reduction priorities. Nevertheless, the premises of market-based PES are being extrapolated as a model for global REDD programmes financed by carbon-offset trading…[T]he contradiction between development and conservation observed in PES is inevitable in projects framed by the asocial logic of neoclassical economics.[112]

REDD also compounds the colonialism of foreign debt. REDD-type Debt for Nature Swaps may be negotiated in Africa as has already occurred in Latin America and Asia."[A] Community forest could be included in debt-for-nature swaps as part of the payment of the foreign debt of the state. In this regard, the United States recently announced that it would subtract US$21 million from the foreign debt of Brazil in exchange for initiatives to protect the forests of the Atlantic Mata in Brazil. Such forest protection could result in REDD-type projects in Brazil."[113] The following summary on a REDD-type "debt-to-aid" deal between the United States and the Philippines is worth reviewing since similar deals will probably be brokered in Africa. The summary also shows how such territorial expropriation for REDD is framed as the United States' generous "help," forest "conservation" and, of course, saving the climate.

"US debt deal helps Philippines save forests
The United States will help preserve the Philippines' rapidly vanishing tropical rainforests under a $31.8-million debt-to-aid conversion signed in Manila on Thursday, the two governments said. Payments on debt owed by the Philippines to the US Agency for International Development will be redirected to starting a tropical forest conservation fund, a joint statement said. The fund would provide grants to conserve, maintain and restore still substantial forest lands in five regions of the archipelago. 'In addition to helping to preserve the Philippines' extraordinary terrestrial biodiversity, the fund will contribute to international climate change mitigation efforts,' the statement said. US-based environment group Conservation International lists the Philippines as one of 17 'mega-diversity' countries that together have more than two-thirds of earth's plant and animal species."[114]

Much remains to be done to have a complete panorama of REDD in Africa and the state of play is constantly changing. REDD's scope has expanded from forests and plantations to include genetically modified (GMO) trees, soils and agriculture. With names like Climate Smart Agriculture, Landscape REDD, Blue Carbon, and Wet Carbon, REDD now covers almost all land and water ecosystems – almost all of Mother Earth's skin, according to the NO REDD+! in RIO+20 – A Declaration to Decolonize the Earth and the Sky of the Global Alliance against REDD.[115] "Ultimately, REDD may try to include and expropriate the entire surface of the Earth including most of the forests, soils, fields, grasslands, deserts, wetlands, mangroves, marine algae and oceans to use them as sponges for industrialized countries' pollution. REDD is also the pillar of the Green Economy. Executive Secretary to the UNFCCC, Christiana Figueres, told delegates gathered at Forest Day on 4 December, that "The governments of the world are writing a global business plan for the planet, [...] and REDD is its spiritual core." [116] REDD turns the sources of life on Earth into carbon garbage dumps.[117] It turns the planet's wombs into tombs. But we are not going to let this happen! Fortunately, resistance is afoot.

18. Colonialism and REDD: The third scramble for Africa?

Stopping the Continent Grab and the REDD-ification of Africa is part of the overall resistance of Africa to colonialism, capitalism, imperialism, the "Green Economy" and mal-development of the post-2015 Development Agenda. This challenge entails countering the exacerbated exploitation of Africa and Africans, the post-2015 "underdevelopment" agenda, and the "decarbonization" of the global economy which will probably be enshrined in the 2015 Paris Accord. It also involves confronting the resurrection of the World Trade Organization, the global carbon market and mandatory offsets, which are fundamental for REDD and the Green Economy.

Since REDD has been denounced as carbon colonialism or even carbon imperialism, it is useful to situate resistance to REDD in the rich history of resistance to and critique of colonialism and imperialism in Africa. In *How Europe Underdeveloped Africa*, Walter Rodney says: "The phenomenon of neo-colonialism cries out for extensive investigation in order to formulate the strategy and tactics of African emancipation and development." [118] The same could be said about REDD.

The Third Scramble for Africa?

The First Scramble for Africa was, of course, the colonial carving up of the continent. The first phase of the Second Scramble was what Kwame Nkrumah called neo-colonialism and Julius Nyerere defined as 'Africans fighting Africans'. Are we now entering a Third Scramble for Africa with the "Green Economy" and REDD?

Perhaps Kwame Nkrumah was too optimistic when in 1965 he dubbed neo-colonialism the "last phase" of imperialism in his book *Neo-Colonialism, the Last Stage of Imperialism*,[119] or perhaps REDD is just the newest chapter in

64

that last phase.

> The neo-colonialism of today represents imperialism in its final and perhaps its most dangerous stage. The essence of neo-colonialism is that the State which is subject to it is, in theory, independent and has all the outward trappings of international sovereignty. In reality its economic system and thus its political policy is directed from outside...

The Mechanisms of Neo-Colonialism:

> ...Faced with the militant peoples of the ex-colonial territories in Asia, Africa, the Caribbean and Latin America, imperialism simply switches tactics. Without a qualm it dispenses with its flags, and even with certain of its more hated expatriate officials. This means, so it claims, that it is 'giving' independence to its former subjects, to be followed by 'aid' for their development. Under cover of such phrases, however, it devises innumerable ways to accomplish objectives formerly achieved by naked colonialism. It is this sum total of these modern attempts to perpetuate colonialism while at the same time talking about 'freedom', which has come to be known as neo-colonialism. The submission of most African governments to the political climate agenda of Northern industrialized countries also tends to reflect "the mechanics of neo-colonialism."[120]

The economic stranglehold of the US and Europe and increasingly China and BRICS on African countries plays out vividly in the UN climate negotiations and in REDD discussions in particular. Even Dr. Tewolde Berhan Gebre Egziabher of Ethiopia, who led the charge of the African Union against genetically modified crops in the Convention on Biological Diversity and so eloquently denounced GMOs as colonialist, when approached at the Copenhagen Summit about the urgent need of the African Union to reject REDD, baulked. Unfortunately, the US and Europe have been highly successful at lobbying African capitals to get them to support the hegemonic climate agenda based on carbon trading.

The historic debates among African leaders like Kwame Nkrumah and Julius Nyerere, and even among Ernesto "Che" Guevara, Samora Machel and fifty others in Dar es Salaam 1965, about whether the priority for Africa was independence or defeating capitalism, and whether African unity was necessary for achieving either of these aspirations, are questions that endure. One may wonder whether these leaders ever imagined a form of colonialism like REDD and how they might have responded. In contrast, the current lack of any African government's outright opposition to REDD is sobering and is indicative of how much African leadership has changed in the last 50 years.

The short note, *Wielding the Power of Vision and Naming to Halt Sky-ocide and Carbon Imperialism,* tried to grapple with the challenges of terminology for the struggle against REDD and the defense of the Sky. [121] "[L]anguage for describing what is happening is so sorely lacking that many are blinded by the blizzard of lies about the true extent, causes of and solutions to this unprecedented planetary catastrophe. One can't help but wonder if carbon colonialism is a more accepted term because uttering the word imperialism is considered too incendiary, off-putting or dated. If that is the case, does using a more palatable term sacrifice accuracy and limit or derail strategic responses?"

Contextualizing and comparing REDD to past systems of domination and exploitation of Africa and Africans, and the corresponding resistance and strategies for emancipation is not a futile or abstract exercise. The hope is that it may help to assess and create possibilities for stopping REDD and the continent grab by comparing not just the phenomena, but the correlation of forces as well as the conditions, structures, economic, material and human resources, consciousness and leadership for resistance.

19. Comparison of colonialism and REDD

The table below provides an outline of the similarities and differences between colonialism and REDD. There is significant overlap and similarities in terms of vast territorial expropriation, *aka* "land grabs", reformatting and commodification of nature and labor, as well as the role, benefits and profits for Northern markets. Land grabs is a term that depoliticizes and renders invisible the perpetrators and victims of territorial expropriation and the geopolitical and economic motives driving the takeover of land. The term evokes a baby grabbing food and, hence, infantilizes a neocolonialist or imperialist endeavor, often more aptly described as expropriation or invasion. Racism goes hand and hand with colonialism and may be part of REDD. According to "NO REDD+! in RIO+20 – A Declaration to Decolonize the Earth and the Sky of the Global Alliance of Indigenous Peoples and Local Communities on Climate Change against REDD+:

> Just as historically the Doctrine of Discovery was used to justify the first wave of colonialism by alleging that Indigenous Peoples did not have souls, and that our territories were *"terra nullius,"* land of nobody, now the Green Economy and REDD+ are inventing similarly dishonest premises to justify this new wave of colonialization and privatization of nature. Indigenous Peoples and peasants are being killed, forcibly relocated, criminalized, and blamed for climate change. Our land is being labeled "unused," "degraded" or in need of "conservation" and "reforestation," to justify massive land grabs for REDD+, carbon offset projects and biopiracy."[122]

Further comparative analysis of how colonialism and REDD reformat nature would be helpful. Such analysis would shed light on how in distinct historical eras, aspects and processes of nature such as land or the atmosphere's carbon cycle are appropriated, converted into capital and new markets, thus creating new kinds of relationships among humans and nonhumans, and even with the air that we breathe.

REDD and the Green Economy commodify all of nature and natural processes turning them into "environmental goods and services". REDD promoters and investors are not all from Europe or the United States, but also hail from the Global South, in particular, from Brazil. In addition, foreign investors are not acting on their own and national political and economic elites are facilitating the expropriation of peasant lands and indirectly engendering hundreds of land conflicts.

Most importantly in terms of stopping REDD and the continent grab, there are major differences with previous struggles against colonialism in terms of the lack of support, allies, funding, training, international instruments, legal framework, UN support, peoples' consciousness, a continental (and global) movement of masses but also the lack of intellectuals and anti-colonialist thinkers applying themselves to REDD and the Green Economy and articulating an analytical framework for resistance. Sadly, there is a disconnect between the magnitude of the systematic and structural threat of REDD and the articulation of resistance.

In the past, colonialism was resisted by peoples and national liberation movements. In the case of REDD, only a few individual communities are trying to defend their human rights and land tenure. Obviously we are living in a very different historical moment from when colonialism was fought and independence obtained in Africa. In terms of consciousness, leadership, mass movements, international support, solidarity and allies, there is nothing comparable now.

Let us create a new liberation movement to free us from immoral debt and neo-colonialism. This is one way forward. The other way is through Pan-African unity.

- Julius Nyerere[123]

It is daunting for civil society, social movements and NGOs to take on this anti-colonialist struggle especially when most citizens have yet to realize that REDD even exists. Nonetheless, we can build on past anti-colonialist and independence struggles by framing the struggle against REDD in those terms.

Many times in history, demanding the impossible has been necessary. Now is no exception. With "stubborn hope,"[124] the *No REDD in Africa Network* and the communities and indigenous peoples of the continent invite you to join the resistance to REDD.

Criteria of Comparison	Colonialism	REDD	Notes
Economy	Colonialist	Colonialist - Imperialist Green Capitalism Green Economy Financialization, global carbon market Convergence of global climate, trade and finance regimes	Offset entire global commodities supply chain and energy matrix

Criteria of Comparison	Colonialism	REDD	Notes
Commodities	Land, labor, enslaved persons, gold, crops	- Timber, biodiversity, crops - Creation of new commodities: Environmental goods and services; Goods: Offsets, Life, Nature, Land, Air, Water, Biodiversity Services: Natural processes	But a huge component of REDD is the land grabbed and *in situ* resources: the extraction of the water, fossil fuels, metals and minerals, which may also be for export. Ecuador's REDD-type Socio-Bosque which allows for fossil fuel extraction and mining indicates that African REDD may eventually do the same.
Markets	Northern Countries and companies	Northern Countries and companies, multinational corporations, carbon exchanges	
Reformats and Commodifies Nature	Reformats some of Nature as "raw materials"	Reformats ALL of Nature and natural processes in its entirety into ecosystem goods and services new measurable and saleable commodities.	REDD reformats air, forests, agriculture, wetlands, mangroves and water ecosystems even when it claims to be doing «nothing» to them.
Agriculture format	Plantations	Plantations for carbon credits, timber, crops, agro-fuels	

Criteria of Comparison	Colonialism	REDD	Notes
Private Property Regimes	Some Land as private property	ALL Land, Water, Life and Sky as private property Scope encompasses every thing, being and aspect (even beauty) and every process	
Enforcement of property rights	Enclosure and fences armed guards	Enclosures, fences, armed guards, Satellite surveillance and remote sensors, and militarization	
Colonists	Europeans	Europeans, Norway, US, China , BRICS especially Brazil	African States and Elites complicit
Colonized	States and Peoples of Global South	States? Peoples, Communities of Global South	
Forms of colonization	Continent Grab Invasion, Militarization Slavery	Continent Grab, violence, militarization, slavery, servitude,	
Racist Premise	Racist and religious justifications Doctrine of Discovery, "Terra Nulius," Papal Bulls, etc	Similarly dishonest premises packaged as "halting deforestation' and using "unused land"	
Struggle for	Independence; Liberation; Own government	Defend land tenure and rights	
Forms of Resistance	Political and Armed national peoples' liberation movements	Political and Non-violent small isolated resistance	

Criteria of Comparison	Colonialism	REDD	Notes
Consciousness Spirit	-Consciousness and commitment at historic high -Effervescence	-Lack of awareness -Relative apathy	
Leaders of Resistance	-Several generations including politicians and intellectuals -Many assassinated	Frontline communities, Indigenous Peoples, a few environmentalists and activists of social movements; dispersed and not articulated, very few politicians and intellectuals	
Allies	Other African countries, China, URSS, Cuba United Nations	Very few allies International human rights orgs unresponsive Most NGOs in favor	Social Movements La Via Campesina; some networks
Funders	People, Other African countries, China, URSS, Cuba	Zero	Donors mostly in favor of REDD
Support	People, Other African countries China, URSS, Cuba	Zero	
Training	Other African countries China, URSS, Cuba	Zero	

Criteria of Comparison	Colonialism	REDD	Notes
International Bodies	UN Special Committee on Decolonization FOR NATION STATES not communities or Indigenous Peoples	-UN is promoting REDD (UN-REDD, World Bank, UNEP, UNDP, etc) -Human rights mechanisms unresponsive to denouncing violations i.e. Special Rapporteur on Indigenous Peoples, CERD, etc -African Commission	-UNPFII witch hunted Indigenous Peoples opposed to REDD as radical -Misuse of UNDRIPs for justifying participating in REDD as self-determined development
Legal Framework	International Covenants -Right to Self-Determination	-No instruments against REDD -No jurisprudence established on violations	
Analytical Framework of Resistance	Huge body of thought both African and foreign over several centuries on abolition of slavery, colonialism, capitalism, imperialism, independence, liberation movements; Centuries of struggle, movements and praxis	-In formation; relatively tiny – mostly descriptive of REDD its impacts, and Green Economy -Almost nothing on strategies of resistance Very little struggle explicitly against REDD	

20. References and endnotes

1.   Africans Unite Against New Form of Colonialism: No REDD in Africa Network Born http://no-redd-africa.org/index.php/news/40-africans-unite-against-new-form-of-colonialism-no-redd-in-africa-network-born

2.   https://www.grain.org/article/entries/5322-how-redd-projects-undermine-peasant-farming-and-real-solutions-to-climate-change

3.   For more information, see WRM website section on REDD and publication 10 Things Communities Should Know About REDD, www.wrm.org.uy

4.   See: http://wrm.org.uy/articles-from-the-wrm-bulletin/recommended/10-things-communities-should-know-about-redd-re-launched-with-a-new-introduction/

5.   Cameron, James, Heroes of the Environment – Richard Sandor http://content.time.com/time/specials/2007/article/0,28804,1663317_1663322_1669930,00.html

6.   Reuters http://www.reuters.com/article/idUSTRE57J3BC20090820

7.   Climate Change News, UN finalizes forest protection initiative at Bonn climate talks http://www.climatechangenews.com/2015/06/10/un-finalises-forest-protection-initiative-at-bonn-climate-talks/

8.   Here is the draft decision that will be considered in Paris: Methodological guidance for activities relating to reducing emissions from deforestation and forest degradation and the role of conservation, sustainable management of forests and enhancement of forest carbon stocks in developing countries http://unfccc.int/resource/docs/2015/sbsta/eng/l05.pdf

9.   REDD Monitor, REDD: An Introduction, http://www.redd-monitor.org/redd-an-introduction/

10.   Ibid

11.   Indigenous Environmental Network, REDD= Reaping profits from Evictions, land grabs, Deforestation and Destruction of Biodiversity Plus Plantations and GMO Trees http://www.ienearth.org/REDD/index.html

12.   UNFCCC Decision that allows GMO trees in plantations for afforestation and reforestation. http://unfccc.int/cop9/latest/substa_127.pdf

13.   Dowie, Mark, Conservation Refugees, "Since 1900, more than 108,000 officially protected conservation areas have been established worldwide, largely at the urging of five international conservation organizations. About half of these areas were occupied or regularly used by indigenous peoples. Millions who had been living sustainably on their land for generations were displaced in the interests of conservation" (Overview) https://mitpress.mit.edu/index.php?q=books/conservation-refugees

14.   Carbon Trade Watch, What is REDD?, http://no redd.makenoise.org/

15.   Indigenous Environmental Network, op.cit.

16.   World Rainforest Movement, REDD moves from forests to landscapes: More of the same, just bigger and bigger risk to cause harm, http://wrm.org.uy/articles-from-the-wrm-bulletin/section1/redd-moves-from-forests-to-landscapes-more-of-the-same-just-bigger-and-with-bigger-risk-to-cause-harm/

17.   Shell bankrolls REDD, Indigenous Peoples and environmentalists denounce http://www.redd-monitor.org/2010/09/08/indigenous-environmental-network-and-friends-of-the-earth-nigeria-denounce-shell-redd-project/

18.   Rio Tinto, an international mining company infamous for violating human rights and causing environmental destruction, promotes REDD. http://noredd.makenoise.org/wp-content/uploads/2010/REDDreaderEN.pdf. IUCN – Rio Tinto Facilitated Workshop Summary http://cmsdata.iucn.org/downloads/workshop_summary.pdf. "Carbon Conservation signed a REDD-deal with Rio Tinto in 2007" http://news.mongabay.com/2009/0726-redd_tasmania.html. The Financial Costs of REDD http://cmsdata.iucn.org/downloads/costs_of_redd_summary_brochure.pdf. Rio Tinto: Global Compact Violador http://www.corpwatch.org/article.php?id=622. Rio Tinto: A Shameful history of Human and Labour Rights Abuses http://london-miningnetwork.org/2010/04/rio-tinto-a-shameful-history-of-human-and-labour-rights-abuses-and-environmentaldegradation-around-the-globe/

19.   Indigenous Environmental Network, op.cit

20.   UN-REDD Framework Document http://www.undp.org/mdtf/UN-REDD/docs/Annex-A-Framework-Document.pdf A Poverty Environment Partnership (PEP) Policy Brief, based on the full report Making REDD Work for the Poor (Peskett et al., 2008) www.povertyenvironment.net/pep/

21.   Carbon Trade Watch and Indigenous Environmental Network, Who Benefits from REDD? http://noreddpoped.makenoise.org/who-benefits-from-redd-players-an-power.html

22.   FAO, World's Forest Map, http://foris.fao.org/static/data/fra2010/forest-2010mapwithleg.jpg

23.   Timberwatch, CDM Carbon Sink Plantations, A Case Study in Tanzania http://timberwatch.org/uploads/Draft%20Plantation_Projects_under%20CDM%20-%20Blessing%20&%20Wally(1).pdf

24.   Basta! and Amis de Terre, REDD+ in Madagascar: You Can't See The Wood For The Carbon http://www.criticalcollective.org/?publication=redd-in-madagascar

25.   GLP REDD Report, p. 50 http://start.org/Publications/REDD_Report.pdf

26.   http://www.no-redd-africa.org/index.php/16-redd-players/84-the-worst-redd-type-projects-in-africa-continent-grab-for-carbon-colonialism

27.   Public Radio International, http://www.loe.org/shows/segments.htm?programID=09-P13-00023&segmentID=3

28.   Think Africa, Mar 24, 2011 http://thinkafricapress.com/environment/commodification-kenya-africa-carbon-exchange

29.   Commodity Online, "Carbon credits to replace US $ as global currency" http://www.commodityonline.com/news/carbon-credits-to-replace-us-$-as-global-currency-25893-3-25894.html. Julian Button, Carbon: Commodity Or Currency? The Case For An International Carbon Market Based On The Currency Model http://Www.Law.Harvard.Edu/Students/Orgs/Elr/Vol32_2/Button%20final%20final.Pdf

30.   REDD Monitor, Climate change at the World Bank: "You can imagine a future world where carbon is really the currency of the 21st century"

31.   The Africa Carbon Exchange: the Commodification of the Environment - Kenya opens Africa's first carbon exchange, Beatrice Gachenge, Think Africa, Mar 24, 2011 http://thinkafricapress.com/environment/commodification-kenya-africa-carbon-exchange

32.   Africa Carbon Credit Exchange, Welcome to ACCE http://www.africacce.com/

33.   See Carbon Trading in Africa, Trusha Reddy et al http://www.issafrica.org/uploads/Mono184.pdf

34.   See the section on Snapshots of Carbon Colonialism in Indigenous Peoples' Guide: False Solutions to Climate Change, Indigenous Environmental

Network http://www.earthpeoples.org/CLIMATE CHANGE/Indigenous Peoples Guide-E.pdf

35.   Africa Carbon Forum – 2014 www.africacarbonforum.com African Carbon Forum "is a trade fair and knowledge sharing platform for carbon investments in Africa. It is a place to discuss the latest development in the carbon market and how the Clean Development Mechanism (CDM) and other mitigation mechanisms can be successful in Africa. The Africa Carbon Forum includes matchmaking and deal facilitation sessions where carbon project developers can showcase their projects to investors and carbon buyers." http://africanclimate.net/en/node/7166

36.   UNEP's role in ACF; CDM: Africa Carbon Forum 2014: 2-4 July, Namibia, cdm.unfccc.int/CDMNews/issues/issues/I_BDWRR6BW54WNWPX. The sixth Africa Carbon Forum will take place in Windhoek, Republic of Namibia, on 2-4 July 2014 to support Africa's participation in global carbon markets Jul 14, 2014 · Mail Guardian South Africa 2014-07-11. The African Carbon Forum is a trade fair and knowledge-sharing event to promote.

37.   Firm targets US buyers with African REDD credits, Point Carbon, Published: 20 Jul 2009 19:59 CET

38.   Reuters, Three firms buy 510,000 African carbon credits in H1 2014 Michael Szabo http://www.reuters.com/article/2014/07/09/carbonoffset-africa-deals-idUSL6N0PK3J020140709

39.   Ibid

40.   The Economist: http://www.economist.com/opinion/displaystory.cfm?story_id=13829421

41.   The Economist: "Trading Thin Air" http://www.economist.com/displaystory.cfm?story_id=9217960

42.   Bassey, Nnimmo, To Cook a Continent. Pambazuka Press, Oxford 2012

43.   The Incineration of Africa "Science says that Africa's geo-physical characteristics make it liable to warm up one-and-half times the global average. Any more warming beyond a critical threshold will in the words of the Ambassador Lumumba Di- Aping of Sudan, then Chair of G77, result in the 'incineration of Africa'," warns African Agenda." http://www.socialwatch.org/node/13887

44.   Challenges and Prospects for REDD+ in Africa, p. 50 and 55 http://www.start.org/Publications/REDD_Report.pdf

45.   No REDD+ in Rio+20 – A Declaration to Decolonize the Earth and the Sky, Global Alliance of Indigenous Peoples and Local Communities on Climate Change against REDD and for Life www.no-redd.com

46.   Just like the right of a farm to call itself organic was commodified, privatized and expropriated by the United States Department of Agriculture for agribusiness under the guise of regulating and certifying organic products.

47.   Clear as Mud, Why agriculture and soils should not be included in carbon offset schemes, The Gaia Foundation, April 2011

48.   Rural Women's Assembly of Southern Africa Statement to COP17 Leaders http://ggjalliance.org/node/897 and signs and sashes on hats against soil carbon trading carried by women in civil society march in Durban, South Africa during COP17.

49.   Ibid

50.   Mugo Mugo , Patrick, Africa for Sale: The Land Grab Landmine, http://www.monitor.upeace.org/innerpg.cfm?id_article=877

51.   Rights and Resources International, African land grabs hinder sustainable development, http://www.nature.com/news/african-land-grabs-hinder-sustainable-development-1.9955

52.   Ibid.

53.   Point Carbon, Firms Targets US Buyers with African REDD credits, 20 July 2009 http://www.pointcarbon.com/news/1.1166150

54.   International Institute for Environment and Development, Nhantumbo, Isilda, REDD+ in Mozambique: new opportunity for land grabbers? http://www.iied.org/blogs/redd-mozambique-new-opportunity-for-land-grabbers

55.   REDD for Communities and Forests et al, A one-step guide to making the national REDD strategy more pro-poor http://climatecapacity.org/files/RC%20REDD%20and%20forestry/Tanz_Policy_Brief_Land_Issues_REDD.pdf

56.   See http://www.theecologist.org/News/news_analysis/640908/lack_of_forest_definition_major_obstacle_in_fight_to_protect_rainforests.html

57.   Nhantumbo, Isilda, REDD+ in Mozambique: new opportunity for land grabbers? http://www.iied.org/blogs/redd-mozambique-new-opportunity-for-land-grabbers

58.   http://www.cip.org.mz/bulletin/en/

59.   These may be conservative estimates. There are at least 8,905,978 hectares or 89,059.78 km sq of REDD-type projects that are active, proposed or have been completed in Cameroon. Cameroon has 199,160 km sq of forests, so the area affected by REDD-type projects is 44.7% of Cameroon's forests. Cameroon is 475,442 km sq so the area affected by REDD-type projects is at least 18.7% of the national territory.

60.   Mongabay, Carbon Scam in Liberia "Liberian President Ellen Johnson Sirleaf established a commission investigate a proposed forest carbon credit deal between the West African nation's Forest Development Authority (FDA) and UK-based Carbon Harvesting Corporation, reports Global Witness... which aimed to secure around a fifth of Liberia's total forest area — 400,000 hectares — in a forest carbon concession. Police in London arrested Mike Foster, CEO of Carbon Harvesting Corporation, last week." http://news.mongabay.com/2010/0610-carbon_scam_liberia.html

61.   REDD Monitor, Shift2Neutral's big REDD deal in the Democratic Republic of Congo http://www.redd-monitor.org/2010/08/27/shift2neutrals-big-redd-deal-in-the-democratic-republic-of-congo/

62.   REDD Monitor, Shift2Neutral Agreement in DRC "illegal" http://www.redd-monitor.org/2010/10/06/shift2neutral-agreement-in-dr-congo-illegal/

63.   Dr. Doreen Stabinsky, professor of Global Environmental Politics at the College of the Atlantic in Bar Harbor, Maine September 23, 2014. Comment on CSA and the UN Climate Summit.

64.   La Via Campesina, Call to Durban, http://climate-connections.org/2011/09/09/la-via-campesina-call-to-durban/

65.   Africans Unite against New Form of Colonialism http://bailiffafrica.org/africans-unite-against-new-form-of-colonialism-no-redd-network-born/

66.   NO REDD+! in RIO+20 – A Declaration to Decolonize the Earth and the Sky, Global Alliance of Indigenous Peoples and Local Communities on Climate Change against REDD+ and for Life http://www.redd-monitor.org/2012/06/19/no-redd-in-rio-20-a-declaration-to-decolonize-the-earth-and-the-sky/

67.   McAfee, Kathleen The Contradictory Logic of Global Ecosystem Services Markets http://www.academia.edu/1625838/The_Contradictory_Logic_of_Global_Ecosystem_Services_Markets

68.   Bracking, Sarah, How do Investors Value Environmental Harm/Care? Private Equity Funds, Development Finance Institutions and the Partial Financialization of Nature-based Industries, http://www.sociologywire.com/2012/02/22/how-do-investors-value-environmental-harmcare-private-equity-funds-development-finance-institutions-and-the-partial-financialization-of-nature-based-industries/

69.   The Mercury, Between the devil and the deep blue sea, October 20, 2009 Edition 1

70.   WWF, Feasibility Study: Sustainable Financing of Protected Areas in Mozambique, p.25

71.   Chevallier, R. 2012. Blue Carbon: The Opportunity of Coastal Sinks for Africa. Policy Briefing 59, Governance of Africa's Resources Programme, SAIIA. http://bluecarbonportal.org/?p=9172

72.   Indigenous Environmental Network, in The No REDD Reader http://www.noredd.makenoise.org/

73.   "How to use offsets in your marketing", see especially Climate Change Chocolate http://ecopreneurist.com/2008/09/08/how-to-use-offsets-in-your-marketing/ and Ecosystem Market Place http://ecosystemmarketplace.com/index.php

74.   "Voluntary Carbon Standard (VSC), backed by Geneva-based International Emissions Trading Association, the Climate Group and World Economic Forum, is likely to capture the largest volumes of the global voluntary offset market...The Basel-based Gold Standard Foundation developed a standard for 'gourmet credits'" http://www.icfi.com/Markets/Climate-Change/doc_files/carbon-credits-switzerland.pdf There are also third-party verifiers like the Climate, Community & Biodiversity Alliance. http://www.climate-standards.org/

75.   Abyd Karmali, Managing Director and Global Head of Carbon Markets at Bank of America Merril Lynch http://www.slideshare.net/FinancingForests09/financing-the-worlds-forests-integrating-markets-and-stakeholders3

76.   Brunner, Stephen, "Gourmet credits; refining Swiss carbon cheese", http://www.icfi.com/Markets/Climate-Change/doc_files/carbon-credits-switzerland.pdf

77.   Mozambique review, July 2011, p.24

78. Panda Leaks: The Dark Side of WWF, "The WWF, renowned global nature conservancy brand,greenwashes the ecological crimes of corporations currently destroying the last remaining rainforests and natural habitats on earth; and it accepts their money. This business model of the famous "eco" organization does more to harm nature than to protect it." http://www.amazon.com/PandaLeaks-The-Dark-Side-WWF/dp/1502366541 "Huismann also dug deep into the early history of the world's biggest, most powerful nature conservancy organization and found several skeletons in the closet: the elite secret club known as "The 1001" and a private military commando unit deployed in Africa against big game poachers – and against black African liberation movements." http://www.pandaleaks.org/operation-lock/

79. Feasibility Study: Sustainable Financing of Protected Areas in Mozambique, p. 17-18, WWF, 2010, http://www.wwf.org.mz/

80. Slash and burn: biochar and REDD in DR Congo and Cameroon http://www.redd-monitor.org/2011/12/06/guest-post-slash-and-burn-biochar-and-redd-in-dr-congo-and-cameroon/

81. "The Congo Basin Forest Fund was launched in 2008, with a £100 million (around €116 million) grant from the UK and Norwegian Governments. It is hosted and administered by the African Development Bank. The priorities are formally aligned with those set by the Central African Forest Commission (COMIFAC) and three out of five relate to building capacity for REDD and Payments for Ecosystem Services. CBFF collaborates closely with the UN REDD Programme." Ibid

82. Transnational Institute, Smith, Kevin, "Offsetting Democracy", http://www.tni.org/detail_page.phtml?act_id=18013

83. Feasibility Study: Sustainable Financing of Protected Areas in Mozambique, p. 17-18, WWF, 2010, http://www.wwf.org.mz/

84. Carbon Plus Capital http://www.carbonpluscapital.com/associates

85. Carbon Plus Capital http://www.carbonpluscapital.com/niassa-reserve-mozambique

86. World Bank, Carbon Finance in Africa Matters http://www.worldbank.org/en/news/feature/2011/07/06/carbon-finance-africa-matters

87. REDD+ Partnership (2011), REDD+Partnership Voluntary REDD+ Database UpdatedProgress Report, 11 June 2011, page 6, table 1.

88. See the Climate and Land Use Alliance, a joint funding initiative of the Ford Foundation, the Betty and Gordon Moore Foundation, the David and Lucile Packard Foundation and ClimateWorks: "The projected 2011 budget for the initiatives described in this strategy overview is approximately $32.5 million", www.climateandlandusealliance.org

89. Congo Basin Forest Fund, 2013 Annual Report, p.12 http://www.afdb.org/fileadmin/uploads/afdb/Documents/Evaluation-Reports/Annual_Report_%E2%80%93_Congo_-_Congo_Basin_Forest_Fund_2013_-_CBFF_%E2%80%93_10_2014.pdf

90. No REDD in Africa Network http://no-redd-africa.org/index.php/16-redd-players/84-the-worst-redd-type-projects-in-africa-continent-grab-for-carbon-colonialism

91. The Guardian, World Bank and UN carbon offset scheme 'complicit' in genocidal land grabs – NGOs. Plight of Kenya's indigenous Sengwer shows carbon offsets are empowering corporate recolonisation of the South http://www.theguardian.com/environment/earth-insight/2014/jul/03/world-bank-un-redd-genocide-land-carbon-grab-sengwer-kenya

92. Friends of the Earth International, REDD: Critical questions and myths exposed, www.foei.org/publications

93. REDD Monitor http://www.redd-monitor.org/2013/04/03/launch-of-no-redd-in-africa-network-redd-could-cause-genocide/

94. REDD Monitor. "REDD Safeguard Information Systems: It's about money not upholding rights" http://www.redd-monitor.org/2015/06/02/redd-safeguard-information-systems-its-about-the-money-not-upholding-rights/

95. Lyon Declaration, International Forum of Indigenous Peoples and Local Communities on Climate, 2000.

96. New York Times, In Scramble for Land, Group Says, Company Pushed Ugandans Out http://www.nytimes.com/2011/09/22/world/africa/in-scramble-for-land-oxfam-says-ugandans-were-pushed-out.html?_r=1

97. Carbon Trading, CDM and REDD: New Forms of Violence against Women NOT Women's Empowerment! July 4, 2014 http://no-redd.com/

98. http://www.unwomen.org/lo/news/in-focus/the-united-nations-conference-on-sustainable-development-rio-20/facts-and-figures#sthash.rL-r8qO8O.dpuf

99.   Judy Kipkenda, Communications and Media Officer of the Ogiek Peoples
       Development Programme, during the United Nations Permanent Forum on
       Indigenous Issues, 2014.

100.   Lohmann, Larry, Marketing and Making Carbon Dumps: Commodifi-
       cation, Calculation and Counterfactuals in Climate Change Mitigation
       http://62.164.176.164/d/Marketing_and_Making_Carbon_Dumps.pdf

101.   Lohmann, Larry, interview, October 9, 2015. He refers to the new kinds of
       rent described by Romain Felli in On Climate Rent, University of Gene-
       va, Historical Materialism In: Environment, not Planning: The Neoliberal
       Depoliticisation of Environmental Policy by means of Emissions Trading,
       Accepted for publication in Environmental Politics May 2015

102.   Ramos, Yvonne, Acción Ecológica, Socio Bosque another face of Green
       Capitalism, No REDD Reader, http://noredd.makenoise.org/wp-content/
       uploads/2010/REDDreaderEN.pdf Max Lascano interview, (May 2010)
       Director of Sociobosque admits drilling for oil and mining are allowed in
       Socio Bosque– Extractive Industries. http://www.youtube.com/watch?v=d-
       PvmqTVX04o

103.   Mining industry eyeing carbon credits http://www.gmanetwork.com/news/
       story/46633/economy/mining-industry-eyeing-carbon-credits

104.   Mining Weekly, SA lagging behind in taking advantage of carbon credits
       system http://www.miningweekly.com/article/sa-lagging-behind-in-taking-
       advantage-of-carbon-credits-system-2008-05-16

105.   See ATTAC TV, Financialization of Nature, video http://www.fame2012.
       org/en/2012/06/15/financialization-nature/ Maryknoll Office for Global
       Concerns, The Financialization of Nature, http://www.maryknollogc.org/
       newsnotes/37.2/Financialization_of_nature.html

106.   REDD Monitor, The Financiali$ation of Nature, http://www.redd-monitor.
       org/2015/08/19/the-financialisation-of-nature/#more-20312

107.   Financialization is a term sometimes used in discussions of financial cap-
       italism which developed over recent decades, in which financial leverage
       tended to override capital (equity) and financial markets tended to dominate
       over the traditional industrial economy and agricultural economics. It is a
       term that describes an economic system or process that attempts to reduce
       all value that is exchanged (whether tangible, intangible, future or present
       promises, etc.) into a financial instrument. The original intent of financial-

ization is to be able to reduce any work-product or service to an exchangeable financial instrument, like currency, and thus make it easier for people to trade these financial instruments (Wikipedia)

108.   Financialization Of Carbon And Biodiversity, Larry Lohmann, Oct 2011

109.   New York Declaration on Forest http://www.un.org/climatechange/summit/wp-content/uploads/sites/2/2014/09/FORESTS-New-York-Declaration-on-Forests.pdf

110.   Global Justice Ecology Project, Timberwatch et al, No REDD papers, volume 1, The REDD+ Trojan Horse, http://www.thecornerhouse.org.uk/sites/thecornerhouse.org.uk/files/No%20REDD%20papers%20One.pdf

111.   A Poverty Environment Partnership (PEP) Policy Brief, Basado en el informe completo "Making REDD Work for the Poor" "(Peskettet al., 2008), p.1 and 2 www.povertyenvironment.net/pep/

112.   McAfee, Kathleen , The Contradictory Logic of Global Ecosystem Services Markets

113.   U.S. signs debt-for-nature swap with Brazil to protect forests, Mongabay.com, August 2010. http://news.monagabay.com/2010/0813-dfns_us_brazil.html

114.   UN debt deal helps Philippines save forests 25 July 2013 http://globalnation.inquirer.net/81527/us-debt-deal-helps-philippines-save-forests

115.   NO REDD+! in RIO+20 – A Declaration to Decolonize the Earth and the Sky, Global Alliance of Indigenous Peoples and Local Communities on Climate Change against REDD+ and for Life http://www.redd-monitor.org/2012/06/19/no-redd-in-rio-20-a-declaration-to-decolonize-the-earth-and-the-sky/

116.   REDD Monitor, News from the Conference of Polluters (Durban, COP 17) http://www.redd-monitor.org/2011/12/08/redd-news-from-the-conference-of-polluters-durban-cop-17-8-december-2011/

117.   World Rainforest Movement, Basureros de Carbono Japoneses en Australia http://www.wrm.org.uy/boletin/27/Australia.html Lohmann, Larry, Marketing and Making Carbon Dumps: Commodification, Calculation and Counterfactuals in Climate Change Mitigation http://62.164.176.164/d/Marketing_and_Making_Carbon_Dumps.pdf

118.   Rodney, Walter, How Europe Underdeveloped Africa, http://www.black-herbals.com/walter_rodney.pdf

119.   Kwame Nkrumah, Neo-Colonialism, the Last Stage of Imperialism," http://www.marxists.org/subject/africa/nkrumah/neo-colonialism/ch01.htm

120.   Ibid

121.   Global Alliance against REDD. Wielding the Power of Vision and Naming to Halt Sky-ocide and Carbon Imperialism, p.1, (Annex II).

122.   Global Alliance of Indigenous Peoples and Local Communities on Climate Change against REDD+, NO REDD+! in RIO+20 – A Declaration to Decolonize the Earth and the Sky http://www.redd-monitor.org/2012/06/19/no-redd-in-rio-20-a-declaration-to-decolonize-the-earth-and-the-sky/

123.   "The Heart Of Africa: Interview With Julius Nyerere On Anti-Colonialism with Ikaweba Bunting", New Internationalist Magazine, Issue 309, January-February 1999

124.   Dennis Brutus, "Stubborn Hope – Selected Poems of South Africa and a Wider World" http://www.unz.org/Pub/BrutusDennis-1979

Appendix 1: Identifying Violations of Indigenous Peoples' Rights by REDD-type Projects

Indigenous Environmental Network

> *The promotion of REDD+ in Chiapas, which the government is doing without consulting us, is causing conflict between our peoples...By failing to consult us, our human rights are violated as well as international agreements such as the United Nations Declaration on the Rights of Indigenous Peoples.-Francisco Hernández Maldonado of the Tseltal People[1]*

By virtue of being indigenous and peoples, Indigenous Peoples have specific collective and individual rights that non-indigenous communities do not enjoy. Indigenous Peoples' rights include the rights recognized and enshrined in the United Nations Declaration on the Rights of Indigenous Peoples (UNDRIPs)[2] and Convention 169 of the ILO.[3] The growing jurisprudence on Indigenous Peoples' rights of United Nations Treaty Bodies[4] is also important as well as that of regional human rights bodies such as the Organization of American States' Inter-American Commission on Human Rights and Inter-American Court of Human Rights, the African Commission on Human and Peoples' Rights, and various European Union human rights mechanisms. An increasing number of States have also incorporated the UN Declaration into their constitutions and systems of law.

Nonetheless, many States continue to patently disregard Indigenous Peoples' rights. In addition, all too often journalists, project proponents, companies, governments, NGOs, consultants and even some United Nations documents and World Bank projects still do not identify Indigenous Peoples as such, but merely refer to them as "populations," "communities," "stakeholders," "minorities," "villagers," "local residents," "small-scale farmers," "immigrants," "workers," "refugees," "victims," "neighbors," "women," "children" or "the poor". "Vulnerable group" is also a much used favorite. Thus

Indigenous Peoples are unwittingly or intentionally rendered invisible, their specific rights are not engaged and the existence or extent of rights violations ignored. This shortcoming is particularly evident in the case of emerging areas of violations of Indigenous Peoples' rights such as carbon trading, the Clean Development Mechanism and the forest carbon offset scheme known as REDD (Reducing Emissions from Deforestation and Forest Degradation).

REDD is mostly being negotiated under the United Nations Framework Convention on Climate Change (UNFCCC). In the UNFCCC negotiations, many States and the United States argue that the United Nations Declaration on the Rights of Indigenous Peoples is only an "aspirational" statement and therefore not legally binding This argument ignores UN Special Procedures reports and findings as well as international jurisprudence, which indicate that the rights of Indigenous Peoples as recognized in the UN Declaration are legally binding, including the right of Free, Prior and Informed Consent. Unfortunately, these same States and others also ignore legally binding international jurisprudence even when it is applied directly to them.

In addition to refusing to apply UNDRIPs to the climate change negotiations, some States try to avoid their human rights obligations by refusing to even recognize Indigenous Peoples within the State. Others recognize Indigenous Peoples only partially, recognizing some peoples and not recognizing others. One State is in the process of deleting all references to Indigenous Peoples from its constitution and law, and now declares that there are no Indigenous Peoples in that State. But States do not create Indigenous Peoples nor can they erase them. Rights apply and must be recognized, protected and implemented regardless of whether States formally recognize the existence of Indigenous Peoples or not. This is especially true in the case of REDD which many fear may result in the biggest land grab of all time and cause genocide.

In its first statement to the United Nations on REDD, the International Forum of Indigenous Peoples on Climate Change, the indigenous caucus to the United

Nations Framework Convention on Climate Change, warned that:

REDD will not benefit Indigenous Peoples, but, in fact, it will result in more violations of Indigenous Peoples' Rights. It will increase the violation of our Human Rights, our rights to our lands, territories and resources, steal our land, cause forced evictions, prevent access and threaten indigenous agriculture practices, destroy biodiversity and culture diversity and cause social conflicts. Under REDD, States and Carbon Traders will take more control over our forests.

The United Nations Declaration on the Rights of Indigenous Peoples... consecrates fundamental rights of Indigenous Peoples which are relevant to the REDD discussions especially Articles 10 [Right to Not be Forcibly Removed], Article 26 [Right to Land, Territory and Resources], Article 27 [Right to Land Tenure Recognition], Article 28 [Right to Redress, Restitution and Compensation], Article 29 [Right to Conservation and Protection of the Environment], Article 30 [Military Activities will not take place in lands or territories] and Article 32 [Right to Development and to determine priorities and strategies for development; Right to Free, Prior and Informed Consent before the approval of any project affecting land, territory and resources].5

In addition, other Indigenous Peoples' rights which may be violated by REDD or REDD-type projects include: Article 18 - Right to Participate in Decision Making, Article 20 - Right to Own Means of Subsistence and Development, Article 2 - Right to be Free of Discrimination, Article 12 - Right to Spiritual Traditions and Sacred Sites, Article 24 - Right to Traditional Medicines, Article 25 - Right to Spiritual Relationship with Land, Territory and Resources, Article 4 - Right to Autonomy and Self-Government and, of course, the crosscutting Article 3 - Right to Self-Determination.

Some of the additional rights violated in the case of REDD-type projects in or near the lands and territories of Indigenous Peoples in Voluntary Isolation or highly vulnerable Indigenous Peoples include Article 7 - Right to Life and Liberty, Article 8 - Right to Not be subjected to Forced Assimilation or Cultural Destruction; Right to Not be Deprived of Integrity as People or Land, Territory or Resources; all of the provisions of the UN Draft Guidelines for the Protection of Indigenous Peoples in Voluntary Isolation[6] as well as Article 2 (c) on "Deliberately inflicting on the group conditions of life calculated to bring about its physical destruction in whole or in part;" of the Convention for the Prevention of Genocide.[7]

Mustering the commitment to fully research and report when Indigenous Peoples are affected by these carbon offset mechanisms is crucial. This quick reference guide is intended to provide a lens to combat the invisibility and cloaking of violations of Indigenous Peoples' rights caused by REDD-type projects, to ensure that the full spectrum of those violations are identified and that the corresponding instruments, standards and remedies are applied.

List of UNDRIPs Articles Frequently violated by REDD-type Projects affecting Indigenous Peoples

Articles 10 [Right to Not be Forcibly Removed], Article 26 [Right to Land, Territory and Resources], Article 27 [Right to Land Tenure Recognition], Article 28 [Right to Redress, Restitution and Compensation], Article 29 [Right to Conservation and Protection of the Environment], Article 30 [Military Activities will not take place in lands or territories] and Article 32 [Right to Development and to determine priorities and strategies for Development; Right to Free, Prior and Informed Consent before the approval of any project affecting land, territory and resources], Article 18 - Right to Participate in Decision Making, Article 20 - Right to Own Means of Subsistence and Development, Article 2 - Right to be Free of Discrimination, Article 12 - Right to Spiritual Traditions and Sacred Sites, Article 24 - Right to Traditional Medicines, Article 25 - Right to Spiritual Relationship with Land, Territory and Resources, Article 4 - Right to Autonomy and Self-Government and the crosscutting Article 3 – Right to Self-Determination.

Additional Articles violated by REDD-type Projects affecting Indigenous Peoples in Voluntary Isolation or Highly Vulnerable Indigenous Peoples

Article 7 - Right to Life and Liberty, Article 8 - Right to Not be subjected to Forced Assimilation or Cultural Destruction; Right to Not be Deprived of Integrity as People or Land, Territory or Resources; all of the provisions of the UN Draft Guidelines for the Protection of Indigenous Peoples in Voluntary Isolation as well as Article 2 (c) on "Deliberately inflicting on the group conditions of life calculated to bring about its physical destruction in whole or in part;" of the Convention for the Prevention of Genocide.

Guidelines:
http://www2.ohchr.org/english/issues/indigenous/ExpertMechanism/2nd/docs/A_HRC_EMRIP_2009_6.pdf
Convention for the Prevention of Genocide
http://www.hrweb.org/legal/genocide.html

Quick Guide to Indigenous Peoples' Rights in the United Nations Declaration on the Rights of Indigenous Peoples

Article 1 - Right to All Rights
Article 2 - Right to be Free of Discrimination
Article 3 - Right to Self-Determination
Article 4 - Right to Autonomy and Self-Government
Article 5 - Right to Own Institutions
Article 6 - Right to Nationality
Article 7 - Right to Life and Liberty
Article 8 - Right to Not be subjected to Forced Assimilation or Cultural Destruction; Right to Not be Deprived of Integrity as People or Land, Territory or Resources
Article 9 – Right to Belong to Community or Nation

Article 10 - Right to Not be Forcibly Removed

Article 11 - Right to Cultural Traditions and Archeological Sites

Article 12 – Right to Spiritual Traditions and Sacred Sites

Article 13 – Right to History and Language

Article 14 – Right to Own Education Systems

Article 15 – Right to have Culture and History reflected in Education Systems

Article 16 - Right to Own Media

Article 17 – Rights of Indigenous Workers

Article 18 – Right to Participate in Decision-Making

Article 19 – Right to Free, Prior, Informed Consent on Laws

Article 20 – Right to Own Means of Subsistence and Development

Article 21 – Right to Improve Economic and Social Conditions

Article 22 – Rights of Indigenous Persons with Disabilities

Article 23 – Right to Development

Article 24 – Right to Traditional Medicines

Article 25 – Right to Spiritual Relationship with Land, Territory and Resources

Article 26 - Right to Land, Territory and Resources

Article 27 – Right to Land Tenure Recognition

Article 28 – Right to Redress, Restitution and Compensation

Article 29 – Right to Conservation and Protection of the Environment

Article 30 – Military Activities will not take place in lands or territories

Article 31 – Right to Cultural Heritage, Traditional Knowledge, Human and Genetic Resources, and Intellectual Property

Article 32 – Right to Development and to determine priorities and strategies for development; Right to Free, Prior and Informed Consent before the approval of any project affecting land, territory and resources

Article 33 – Right to Identity and Membership

Article 34 – Right to Institutional Structures

Article 35 – Right to Determine Responsibilities of Individuals to Community

Article 36 – Right to Cross Borders (for transboundary peoples)

Article 37 – Rights to Treaties

Article 38 - Appropriate Measures to Achieve this Declaration

Article 39 – Assistance for the Enjoyment of Rights

Article 40 – Effective Remedies

Article 41 – UN to contribute to full realization of Declaration

Article 42 – UN and Permanent Forum to promote full application

Article 43 – Declaration as Minimum Standard

Article 44 – Rights equally granted to males and females

Article 45 – Declaration does not diminish or extinguish present or future rights

Article 46 – Territorial Integrity of States and limitations

(Endnotes)

1 Francisco Hernández Maldonado, an indigenous Tzeltal *Representative (Comisariado Ejidal) of the Community Amador Hernández in* the Lacandon Jungle of Chiapas, Mexico, submission to the California Air Resources Board http://climate-connections.org/2011/08/23/environmental-indigenous-peoples-and-human-rights-groups-reject-international-offsets-in-californias-global-warming-solutions-act/

2 http://www.un.org/esa/socdev/unpfii/en/drip.html Also annexed to this document.

3 http://www.ilo.org/indigenous/Conventions/no169/lang--en/index.htm

4 For example, the International Covenant on Civil and Political Rights http://www2.ohchr.org/english/law/ccpr.htm   International Covenant on Economic, Social and Cultural Rights http://www2.ohchr.org/english/law/cescr.htm Clearly, the International Convention on the Elimination of all forms of Racial Discrimination (CERD),   http://www2.ohchr.org/english/law/cerd.htm the Convention on the Elimination of all forms of Discrimination against Women (CEDAW) http://www.un.org/womenwatch/daw/cedaw/text/econvention.htm and the Convention on the Rights of the Child http://www2.ohchr.org/english/law/crc.htm are all also relevant.

5 International Forum of Indigenous Peoples on Climate Change, UNFCCC, COP13, December 2007, Bali, Indonesia, SBSTA 27, agenda item 5/REDD, International Alliance of Indigenous and Tribal Peoples on the Tropical Forests

http://www.international-alliance.org/documents/IFIPCC%20Statement%20on%20
REDD.doc

6 See http://www2.ohchr.org/english/issues/indigenous/ExpertMechanism/2nd/
docs/A_HRC_EMRIP_2009_6.pdf

7 http://www.hrweb.org/legal/genocide.html

Appendix 2: Violation of Free, Prior and Informed Consent by UN-REDD and REDD

Of the sixteen countries with UN-REDD National Programmes, at least ten countries have violated the right to free, prior and informed consent and the right to participation of civil society and Indigenous Peoples in processes related to REDD.

Country (Yellow indicates countries with UN-REDD national programme)	Free, prior, informed consent	Other abuses related to REDD	Sources
LATIN AMERICA			
Brazil (California REDD)	NO	"neocolonialist proposal" http://www.redd-monitor.org/2013/04/29/letter-from-brazil-opposing-redd-in-californias-global-warming-solutions-act-ab32/#more-13816	Open Letter rejecting California REDD http://www.redd-monitor.org/2013/04/29/letter-from-brazil-opposing-redd-in-californias-global-warming-solutions-act-ab32/#more-13816 Declaration of Solidarity http://www.redd-monitor.org/2013/05/01/declaration-of-solidarity-with-the-letter-from-acre-brazil-opposing-redd-offset-credits-in-californias-cap-and-trade-scheme/#more-13828
Bolivia			

Ecuador	**NO**	Oil Drilling and Mining allowed in Socio Bosque http://www.youtube.com/watch?v=dPvmqT-VX04o	CONIAE – Letter to UN and Ban Ki-Moon demanding cancelation of all REDD projects in Ecuador., REDD Papers, Volume 1, http://climatevoices.files.wordpress.com/2011/11/noreddpapers_download.pdf Indigenous Peoples in Ecuador reject REDD http://www.redd-monitor.org/2009/08/11/indigenous-peoples-in-ecuador-reject-redd/
El Salvador (World Bank REDD)	**NO**		REDD Monitor http://www.redd-monitor.org/2012/06/05/indigenous-peoples-in-el-salvador-reject-the-world-banks-fcpf/ http://www.redd-monitor.org/2012/05/17/social-organisations-in-el-salvador-critique-the-world-banks-fcpf/#more-12497
Guyana	**NO**	"failure to uphold land rights" "lack of transparency"	In Guyana, for example, the verification body for the Guyana-Norway MoU on REDD+ found in November 2012 that after three years Guyana has failed to take suitable actions to uphold indigenous peoples land rights, while ineffective public consultations and a lack of transparency continue to plague the development of sustainable REDD+ policies in the country.[9] http://www.redd-monitor.org/2013/05/01/concerns-grow-over-weak-safeguard-implementation-forest-peoples-programme-on-redd-and-safeguards/#more-13827
Honduras (World Bank REDD)	**NO**		CONPINH a Banco Munidal http://bit.ly/ZTDomN
Mexico (California REDD)	**NO**		Open Letter rejecting California REDD - Carta Abierta rechazando REDD de california http://reddeldia.blogspot.mx/2013/04/carta-abierta-de-chiapas-sobre-el.html

Panama	NO		COONAPIP se retira de ONU-REDD http://www.redd-monitor.org/2013/03/06/coonapip-panamas-indigenous-peoples-coordinating-body-withdraws-from-un-re-dd/ Central American Indignous Council raises concerns of Racial Intolerance and Discrimination http://www.redd-monitor.org/2013/03/20/central-american-indige-nous-council-raises-concerns-of-racial-intol-erance-and-discrimination-in-un-redd/
Paraguay	NO		World Bank approves R-PIN for Par-aguay despite lack of consultation with Indigenous Organisations http://www.redd-monitor.org/2008/11/14/world-bank-approves-r-pin-for-para-guay-despite-lack-of-consultation-with-in-digenous-organisations/
Peru	NO	-Promises to demarcate territory not fulfilled -AIDESEP considering presenting a complaint	In Peru, the Amazonian indigenous organi-sation AIDESEP has growing concerns over the treatment of rights and land issues in the the the process to develop a national Forest Investment Strategy financed by the For-est Investment Programme (FIP). In short, AIDESEP has been dismayed that **previous pledges to address land tenure with adequate national budgets for demar-cation and titling were broken when the government unilaterally redraft-ed the investment plan without con-sultation** at the start of 2013. AIDESEP is now considering use of various complaints mechanisms if its safeguard concerns are not addressed.[8]

Suriname	**NO**		In countries like Suriname, despite repeated redrafting of national readiness proposals, government plans for REDD+ continue to omit any meaningful measures to uphold the land and territorial rights of forest peoples.[5]
ASIA			
Cambodia			
Indonesia	**NO**	-	Friends of the Earth International, *In the REDD, Australia's Carbon Offset Projects in Central Kalimantan,* http://www.foei.org/en/resources/publications/pdfs/2011/in-the-redd-australias-carbon-offset-project-in-central-kalimantan
Papua New Guinea	**NO**		REDD Projects in Papua New Guinea legally untenable http://www.redd-monitor.org/2010/09/14/redd-projects-in-papua-new-guinea-legally-untenable/
Philippines			
Sri Lanka			
Vietnam	**NO**		ONU-REDD "admits that FPIC processes in Vietnam have been flawed (failing to explain risks and costs of REDD+ to communities). In the programme's pilot REDD+ project in Central Sulawesi in Indonesia, locals complain that no meaningful FPIC process has yet taken place." http://www.redd-monitor.org/2013/05/01/concerns-grow-over-weak-safeguard-implementation-forest-peoples-programme-on-redd-and-safeguards/#more-13827

AFRICA			
Nigeria	**NO**	Criminalization of activist Odey Oyama of Cross River, UN-REDD and World Bank REDD area	No REDD in Africa Network http://www.redd-monitor.org/2013/05/04/no-redd-in-africa-network-opposes-inclusion-of-redd-offsets-in-californias-cap-and-trade-scheme/#more-13860
Republic de Congo	**NO**	"lack of transparency and inadequate participation"	"The participants also denounced the lack of transparency and inadequate participation of forest-dependent communities in the multiple new initiatives designed to support REDD in the Congo Basin, including the World Bank's Forest Carbon Partnership Facility (FCPF) and the United Nations' REDD programme.." http://www.redd-monitor.org/2008/11/30/forest-communities-of-the-congo-basin-speak-out-on-redd-moving-the-debate-beyond-financing/#more-688

Democratic Republic of Congo	**NO**	Civil society withdrew from World Bank REDD	GTCR Civil society groups in DRC suspend engagement with National REDD Coordination Process 23 July, 2012 In late June civil society organizations tracking REDD+ policies in the Democratic Republic of Congo (DRC) sent open letters to the World Bank's Forest Carbon Partnership Facility (FCPF) and to the DRC's Environment Minister expressing grave concerns about the lack of effective public and community participation in national REDD+ policy-making (see links below this article). The "REDD Climate Working Group" (GTCR), which authored the letters and is composed of a broad range of national and local environment and development NGOs in DRC, is insisting on the reorganisation of REDD governance structures in DRC to ensure decentralisation and ensure meaningful participation by civil society and forest peoples in forest and climate policy making at all levels.
Tanzania	**NO**		More Corruption involving Norwegian REDD Funding in Tanzania http://www.redd-monitor.org/2013/02/06/more-corruption-involving-norwegian-redd-funding-in-tanzania/
Zambia			
PACIFIC			
Solomon Islands			

Appendix 3: South-South REDD: A Brazil-Mozambique Initiative – Of "Pan-African Relevance"

South-South REDD: A Brazil-Mozambique Initiative, is a model national REDD strategy with "pan-African relevance"[1] implemented in Mozambique based on the Brazilian Amazon Fund, the Bolsa Floresta program and the Juma pilot REDD project. It seems to be the prototype for the South-South: Brazil-Africa Initiative for promoting REDD with fifteen African countries (probably including, in addition to Mozambique, Central African Republic, Cameroon, Democratic Republic of Congo, Gabon, Madagascar and the Republic of Congo[2] among others).

The Amazon Fund for promoting REDD in the Brazilian Amazon was created with a billion dollar donation from Norway and is managed by the Brazilian National Bank (BNDES). Critics of the Amazon Fund are quick to point out that the BNDES funds megaprojects and agrofuels in the Amazon which are major drivers of deforestation. Norway's funding has also been denounced as greenwash for the major contract between the Norwegian state oil company, Statoil, and Petrobras to drill for oil offshore which could have a devastating impact on the environment and livelihoods of communities of Brazil's stunning coast.[3] In view of this flimsy front for destructive extractive industries and a bank that funds deforestation, the Amazon Fund is not a particularly encouraging REDD model for Africa.

The Bolsa Floresta program has a number of different payment components. (See below.) It seems sort of like a REDD form of welfare which could create dependency and dollarize indigenous and local cultures. One of the biggest concerns about *Bolsa Floresta Familiar*, which pays families USD$25 a month with an ATM debit card in exchange for not deforesting nor practicing traditional agriculture, is that the money from Bolsa Floresta may be less than the value of subsistence and caloric intake derived from free access to the forest. If this is the case, REDD could be already causing malnutrition and even hunger.

There is a brief interview with an indigenous woman in Mark Shapiro' PBS video[4] about the Juma Project and the Bolsa Floresta payments. In it, the woman explains that half of the money is used for gasoline to travel down river each month to go to the ATM machine. Her husband hangs out in the background and has been prohibited from doing agriculture. When asked if the Bolsa Floresta payments are sufficient, the woman says "No." However, there are conflicting reports about whether other community members are pleased with the program or not. A complete, independent evaluation of the the Juma Project and Bolsa Floresta would be extremely useful for Mozambican civil society to strategize on their response to South-South REDD Initative and would probably eventually be useful for other countries in Africa in the South-South: Brazil-Africa Initiative, too.

Here is the description in Portuguese of South-South REDD: A Brazil-Mozambique Initiative:

COOPERAÇÃO SUL-SUL SOBRE REDD UMA INICIATIVA MOÇAM-BIQUE-BRASIL PARA O DESMATAMENTO ZERO COM RELEVÂNCIA PAN-AFRICANA p.5 http://pubs.iied.org/pdfs/G02605.pdf No Brasil, a Fundação Amazonas Sustentável (FAS) possui experiência no planeamento eimplementação de mecanismos de pagamentos por serviços ambientais, at-ravés do Programa

Bolsa Floresta (PBF). O PBF visa beneficiar financeiramente as famílias e comunidades residentes nas Unidades de Conservação do Estado do Amazonas que se comprometem a realizar acções para reduzir a zero o desmatamento. O PBF começou como um programa estatal do Governo do Amazonas e agora é administrado pela FAS. Actualmente, os pagamentos já beneficiam mais de 6.000 famílias em 14 Unidades de Conservação, cobrindo mais de 10 milhões de hectares. O PBF possui uma série de características exclusivas, as quais garantem a sua abordagem rigorosa na busca do 'desmatamento zero'. A estrutura do programa está dividida em quatro componentes, criando um equilíbrio nos incentivos que fazem que a busca pelo 'desmatamento zero' seja atractiva economicamente para as *famílias e comunidades. As componentes estão descritas a seguir: (i) Bolsa Floresta Familiar: pagamento directo através de uma recompensa mensal às famílias participantes (US$25,00 por mês) na qual a distribuição do dinheiro é realizada através da utilização de um cartão de débito para saque, num sistema administrado por um banco popular do Brasil (Bradesco). Para receber o benefício, as famílias assinam um acordo com o Governo do Estado comprometendo-se a não desmatar florestas primárias nas reservas em que moram. A FAS e o Governo são os responsáveis pelo monitoramento do desmatamento dentro das reservas; (ii) Bolsa Floresta Associação – pagamento directo às associações das comunidades visando fortalecer a governação local e a participação de interessados (equivalente a 10% da soma do montante destinado às famílias – aproximadamente US$500,00 por mês); (iii) Bolsa Floresta Renda – investimento na produção sustentável das comunidades, sem queimadas, baseada no maneio de recursos naturais (US$175,00 por ano, multiplicado pelo número de famílias. Em média, US$70.000 por área protegida por ano); (iv) Bolsa Floresta Social – destinado às comunidades para investimento na melhoria da saúde, educação, comunicação e transporte (US$175,00 por ano multiplicado pelo número de famílias. Em média, US$70.000 por área protegida por ano). A FAS é também responsável pela coordenação e implementação do Projecto de REDD da RDS do Juma, o primeiro projecto de REDD do Brasil, certificado de acordo com os critérios do CCBA (Climate, Community and Biodiverstiy) pela TUV-SUD e também o primeiro do mundo a obter o nível ouro de qualidade.*

A provisional list of participants of South-South: A Brazil-Mozambique Initiative includes major national and international players like several ministries of the Government of Mozambique, IUCN, the World Bank, Norway, Indufor, a plantation company, and WWF.

At the Copenhagen climate summit, Indufor prepared a side event at which members of the Mozambican delegation together with FAS would present the South-South REDD initiative and the roadmap towards a national action plan for REDD+.

As for the pilot projects that South-South is working on, they include "plantation establishment," which has been an extremely contentious and even conflictive issue in Mozambique in recent years and intimately linked to large-scale land grabs. Pilot areas in order of priority include in "Chicualalacua-Mabalane-Guija in Gaza; buffer Zone of the Gorongoza National Park in Sofala; Mecuburi District in Nampula and Chipanje Chetu in Niassa." There is also interest in "what might be eligible for REDD+ funding in each of the main sectors: Environment, Agriculture, Forestry, Energy, Mining [?!] and Infrastructure development," "a tax channelled toward forest and agroforestry establishment" and something called the 'one leader one forest' initiative.

South-South includes efforts to overhaul the legal framework of Mozambique to make it easier to implement REDD and implicitly to grab land. "The chapter also describes how current legislation paves the way for REDD+, notably through the Land Law (1997), the Environmental Law (1997) the Forest and Wildlife Law (1999) and subsequent regulation (2002)." There is also enthusiasm to "develop carbon rights legislation" and "promote community tenure and use rights – including over carbon." It is very important not to be fooled by the REDD discourse of promoting land rights for communities. The only reason that community land rights are being given attention is to be able to get the rights to the carbon and the land for REDD implementation. The report on the *Financial Costs of REDD*[5] prepared by IUCN and funded by the infamous mining company Rio Tinto (which is also active in Mozambique) seems to suggest that it is much cheaper to do REDD by providing communities and indigenous peoples their land rights on the condition that they do REDD, than paying soy plantation barons or loggers not to deforest. It is beyond ironic that if a community "gets" its land rights through REDD, the REDD project itself will probably prohibit the exercise of those rights (i.e. by outlawing traditional agriculture or restricting access to the land itself.) Achieving community land rights through REDD is a highly deceptive myth and needs to be debunked especially since so many indigenous peoples' organizations and even national movements are being tricked in this regard.

For the peasants of Mozambique, it is relevant that South-South plans to increase "agricultural productivity including both 'green revolution' and 'conservation agriculture' approaches" as part of its REDD work. This smacks of agro-business for REDD credits and requires further monitoring and research.

Paradoxically, South-South tips its hat to the REDD safeguards that do not save. "This issue also brings the importance of safeguards, ensuring that REDD+ and indeed CDM projects such as those involved in large scale plantations seeking access to carbon credits do not result in more harm (to the people, State and resources) than good." Given what we know about plantations' social and environmental impacts, these sound like empty aspirations indeed.

---

1 Cooperação Sul-Sul Sobre Redd Uma Iniciativa Moçambique - Brasil Para O Desmatamento Zero Com Relevância Pan-Africana http://pubs.iied.org/pdfs/G02605.pdf

2 **FCPF, GEF Organize Brazil-Africa Event on REDD+ and Community Forestry http://climate-l.iisd.org/news/fcpf-gef-organize-brazil-africa-event-on-redd-and-community-forestry/**

3 See *Extractive Industries and REDD* in the *No REDD! Reader* http://www.noredd.makenoise.org/

4 PBS/Frontline World, Carbon Watch, Centre for Investigative Journalism http://www.pbs.org/frontlineworld/stories/carbonwatch/moneytree/

5 *Financial Costs of REDD: Evidence from Brazil and Indonesia* http://cmsdata.iucn.org/downloads/costs_of_redd_summary_brouchure.pdf

Appendix 4: Resources for analysis and action

This appendix provides a list of resources that you may wish to refer to, in addition to the references to be found in the references and endnotes.

No REDD in Africa Documents

- Africans Unite against New Form of Colonialism: No REDD Network Born http://no-redd-africa.org/index.php/news/40-africans-unite-against-new-form-of-colonialism-no-redd-in-africa-network-born
- The No REDD in Africa Maputo Declaration http://no-redd-africa.org/index.php/declarations/42-maputo-statement-no-redd-in-africa-network-declaration-on-redd
- Worst REDD-Type Projects in Africa http://no-redd-africa.org/index.php/16-redd-players/84-the-worst-redd-type-projects-in-africa-continent-grab-for-carbon-colonialism

WEBSITES

No REDD http://no-redd.com
No REDD In Africa Network http://no-redd-africa.org/
Carbon Trade Watch http://www.carbontradewatch.org/
No REDD Make Noise http://no redd.makenoise.org/
World Rainforest Movement http://wrm.org.uy/?s=REDD
REDD Monitor http://www.redd-monitor.org/

VIDEOS

Exposing REDD http://www.redd-monitor.org/2012/10/30/new-video-exposing-redd-the-false-climate-solution/

Darker Shade of Green – REDD Alert http://climate-connections.org/tag/a-darker-shade-of-green/

Money Tree PBS/Frontline World, Carbon Watch, Centre for Investigative Journalism http://www.pbs.org/frontlineworld/stories/carbonwatch/moneytree/

The Story of Cap and Trade, Annie Leonard https://www.youtube.com/watch?v=pA6FSy6EKrM

PUBLICATIONS

REDD = Reaping profits from Evictions, land grabs, Deforestation and Destruction of biodiversity. Indigenous Environmental Network, http://www.ienearth.org/REDD/index.html

The No REDD Reader http://noredd.makenoise.org/wp-content/uploads/2010/REDDreaderEN.pdf

The No REDD Papers, volume 1 http://no-redd.com/no-redd-papers/

Why is REDD happening? What is REDD? Who benefits from REDD? Players and Power, Carbon Trade Watch http://noreddpoped.makenoise.org/

Ten Things Communities should know about REDD, World Rainforest Movement http://wrm.org.uy/wp-content/uploads/2013/01/10_Alerts_REDD_to_print_small_eng1.pdf

REDD moves from Forests to Landscapes, World Rainforest Movement http://wrm.org.uy/articles-from-the-wrm-bulletin/section1/redd-moves-from-forests-to-landscapes-more-of-the-same-just-bigger-and-with-bigger-risk-to-cause-harm/

REDD Myths, Friends of the Earth International, http://www.foei.org/en/resources/publications/pdfs/2008/redd-myths

Shell bankrolls REDD http://www.redd-monitor.org/2010/09/08/indigenous-environmental-network-and-friends-of-the-earth-nigeria-denounce-shell-redd-project/

Carbon Trading – How It Works And Why It Fails, Carbon Trade Watch. http://www.carbontradewatch.org/publications/carbon-trading-how-it-works-and-why-it-fails.html

Carbon Trading in Africa: A Critical Review http://www.carbontradewatch.org/publications/carbon-trading-in-africa-a-critical-review.html

Dozen of the Worst REDD-type Projects Affecting Indigenous Peoples and Local Communities http://www.ienearth.org/docs/REDD-A%20Dozen-of-the-Worst-REDD-type-projects.pdf

Cashing in on Creation: Gourmet REDD privatizes, packages, patents, sells and corrupts all that is Sacred, Indigenous Environmental Network, The No REDD Reader http://www.noredd.makenoise.org/

When 'payment for environmental services' delivers a permit to destroy, World Rainforest Movement http://www.wrm.org.uy/html/wp-content/uploads/2014/04/Trade-in-Ecosystem-Services.pdf

Economic Valuation of Nature, The Price to Pay for Conservation?, Rosa Luxembourg Foundation http://rosalux-europa.info/userfiles/file/Economic-Valuation-of-Nature.pdf